CONVERSATIONS
with
TAIICHI OHNO

Management Insights
for the Digital Age

BOB EMILIANI

Conversations with Taiichi Ohno: Management Insights for the Digital Age / Bob Emiliani

Cover design and illustration by Bob Emiliani
Cover font: Classic Robot by Neale Davidson, Pixel Sagas
Interior font: Garamond

ISBN-13: 978-0-9898631-8-6
Library of Congress Control Number: 2017941107

1. Business 2. Management 3. Economics
4. Toyota Production System 5. Digital Transformation
6. Information Age

First Edition: June 2017

Published by The CLBM, LLC, South Kingstown, Rhode Island, USA

This book is a fictional account of conversations between the author and a deceased person. It is believed to convey reasonably accurate information with respect to the subject matter covered, though many errors are likely. It is sold with the understanding that it does not in any way represent legal, financial, business, consulting, or other professional service. Buyer of this book assumes all risks.

Manufactured using digital print-on-demand technology.

CONTENTS

Taiichi Ohno (1912-1990)

Preface

Why write a fictional account of conversations with Taiichi Ohno (1912-1990), who, with his team, created the ever-evolving Toyota Production System (TPS)?

As time has gone by, people have lost contact with Taiichi Ohno's writings and, especially, his unique way of thinking. This loss, in turn, results in an inability to establish or even create something similar to TPS, inclusive of the remarkable financial and non-financial results that can be achieved.

It is clear that people have struggled to understand various aspects of TPS. As a result, many variations have been created to simplify TPS so that companies can achieve some positive results – even if results far less than what TPS can deliver. Nearly 30 years after his passing, it is time to again look at Mr. Ohno's work and understand important management details that lie at the core of TPS but were easy for people to miss.

This book seeks to elaborate on and extend Ohno-san's way of thinking to the present time and into the future. Along the way, I hope to illustrate how Ohno-san's way of thinking and TPS are more responsive to the 21st century digital age than it was to the 20th century industrial age.

Fundamentally, this work has the intention of being educational and to guide people towards Ohno-san's way of thinking. It is a way of thinking that has so much good associated with it, from employee development, to customer satisfaction, to company success, to resource conservation, to improving the human condition.

As I am no expert in TPS, my efforts to educate and guide you will surely be flawed in various ways. But, people who allow themselves to be educated and guided along a path have a responsibility, at some point, to think for themselves. Therefore, any shortcomings in this work can be corrected by the reader through diligent effort.

Taiichi Ohno's work proves that we underestimate how difficult it is to learn. A more expedient route is to copy others under the assumption that what they learned is the correct way to do things and, therefore, it is right for us as well. But, if we were to abandon our preconceptions, we would find that this assumption is flawed and much of what we copied is actually the wrong way to do things.

It is easy to make things complex, and, as a result, ensure that people struggle for decades. If, instead, we struggled for a short time in an effort to make things simpler, people would be happy for decades. This is the thought in mind that serves as the basis for this book.

But, making things simple requires the development of a new mindset through teaching, coaching, and practice, much in the way that one learns how to play golf or piano. Sport and music have ways of thinking associated with them that cannot be understood by those who have not practiced them. Amateurs possess limited understanding, while professionals possess much deeper understanding. The mindset that managers have about business offers nothing in the way of TPS mindset. The typical way of thinking about business and TPS are as different as stone and water.

As business professionals, managers should diligently work towards developing deeper understandings of business by studying and practicing TPS. One point of caution: Don't fall under the illusion that the "P" in TPS stands solely for production. Its meaning is broader and encompasses all production and non-production processes. TPS is a management system for the entire company.

In producing this book, my utmost concern has been to respect Mr. Ohno – the man, his work, and his legacy, as well as Toyota and its managers and associates, past, present, and future. I hope I have not failed. I take full responsibility for all content, including the many errors.

Bob Emiliani
South Kingstown, Rhode Island
June 2017

• • • • •

NOTE: Unless I have quoted Taiichi Ohno, he has never actually said anything written in this book. Therefore, do not attribute or quote anything I have written to Taiichi Ohno. Cite relevant passages exactly as follows:

> In the book *Conversations with Taiichi Ohno*, Emiliani imagines Ohno-san to have said: Therefore, managers who reap the rewards of sellers' markets become complacent and are doomed when the shift to buyers' markets eventually comes.

Note the absence of quotation marks after the colon.

Introduction

BE Ohno-san, much has happened over the last 40 years since people first became aware of TPS. During that time, many new interpretations of TPS have been created. People see the various interpretations as true TPS, though they clearly are not. I would like to talk with you about this and related phenomena.

TO What is the purpose to discuss interpretations of TPS that I know nothing about? What is the need? Every business has a different production system. Does it matter if it is the same or different that TPS?

BE I do not want to discuss the different interpretations. Instead, I want to talk about TPS in greater detail. Greater detail than what you have written in *Toyota Production System, Workplace Management*, and *Just-In-Time for Today and Tomorrow* [published in Japanese in 1978, 1982, and 1986, respectively, and in English in 1988]. In this way, people will be able to learn more about TPS. It extends your desire to share TPS with the world in order to develop human capabilities and for the benefit of humanity. I think people will benefit by understanding TPS better.

TO To improve their understanding, they must establish TPS by trial-and-error.

BE I agree. But I believe that discussing various aspects of TPS will help people learn and understand more, which will motivate them to establish TPS through trial-and-error and keep up their efforts. Perhaps I am wrong.

TO This may be true for some people. However, my view is that books put people's mind in a straight-jacket, and books, once published, remain fixed even as times change. I fear my books have had that effect on people. How will you avoid that?

BE There may be no way to avoid it. I would like to expand your thinking on the basics of TPS, so that people can grasp them more easily and apply them more thoroughly.

TO You are foolish to think I did not try to do that. By having this conversation, you are telling me that I did not succeed in presenting the basics. Is that so?

BE Yes and no.

TO Why must I engage in further explanation. I think you should engage in further TPS practice on the genba. That way, you can explain things further without my assistance.

BE That is true.

TO Have there been many books published since mine were published in English?

BE There has. Perhaps 300 or 400 hundred. Maybe more.

TO And what has been the result of all those books, besides publishers profits and author's royalties?

BE A mix of understanding and confusion. More confusion than understanding, it seems. More de-evolution away from TPS than evolution towards TPS among companies not affiliated with Toyota – the ones who seek to adopt TPS or one of its many interpretations.

TO Where there has been understanding, what has been the result?

BE The results have been good. They have achieved good business results and good outcomes for customers and employees and others as well.

TO I see. What does "good" mean?

BE It means that companies have achieved some measure of what Toyota has achieved – but usually only up to the time of your retirement in 1978. Those that have succeeded have struggled to go beyond basic TPS implementation.

TO So, good results are rare. I experienced this as well. But I did not expect such constancy of results over this long period of time – nearly 40 years. I sincerely believe humanity benefits from TPS in innumerable ways. Perhaps the interpretations of TPS do not hold such promise.

BE The interpretations often do not recognize what you would consider to be important. The interpretations picked some things to include and left out other things. Sometimes corrections are made, but often after many years or even decades.

TO I warned people about that.

BE You did, but they did not listen.

TO As you know, I think efforts must be made to reduce people's struggles. Though, TPS is always a struggle, so I am uncertain how such struggles can be reduced.

BE I share your concern. If the benefits of TPS are to be realized more broadly, for humanity and not just for business, then we need to find ways to reduce people's struggles.

TO That may be. However, I am not convinced that more words or another book is needed.

BE I am not convinced either. But I believe we have to try. This book can be viewed as another experiment to influence people so that they will commit to establishing TPS and engage in trystorming on-the-job. I believe in the past you said that a bigger effort must be made to teach people the fundamental nature of TPS.

TO Because of that, and because this is an experiment, I will go along, with the hope that our conversation can be an effective countermeasure for some people. I want you to make this a workbook so that people think about what they read and do a practical exercise. Add a page at the end of each conversation asking how it helped improve their understanding of TPS and reduce their struggles.

BE Thank you. I will do that. I propose that we use the English versions of your three books to guide our conversations.

TO That is acceptable. But, don't believe that everything you read in English is exactly as I said it. Accurate interpretation of Japanese language into English is difficult. Despite this, I am confident that the English interpretations of my books are a useful guide for managers – especially if they try putting the things they read into practice. Also, do not ask me to clarify that which is already clear. I will only discuss what time has proven to be difficult for people to understand. Perhaps this will help reduce their struggles.

BE Thank you very much.

TO Before we begin, please tell the me problem statement. What is the problem you are trying to solve?

BE There are two related problem statements: 1. Managers have great difficulty understanding TPS. Therefore, they do not consider TPS or they struggle to establish TPS and typically fail. 2. Because of 1, managers do not consider TPS as a management system for the digital age. I propose we address problem statement one in Day 1, 2, and 3 of our conversations and problem statement two in Day 4 and 5 of our conversations.

TO Very well, proceed.

Day One
Conversation

Sellers' and Buyers' Markets

BE As I read your writings, I find that you are very clear in stating that the days of selling whatever one can make have long been over, and that companies must meet the individual needs of customers. TPS is a method for doing that.

TO Why are we talking about something that is clear? I said I did not want to talk about that.

BE I would like to explore this subject because, remarkably, it is unclear to others. It is a powerful example of how people can miss critically important information in a book. The market basis for the creation of TPS is fundamental to what people are trying to achieve. If they don't understand that, then they achieve results independent of actual needs.

TO Why is this my concern? People should read my books more than once if they cannot comprehend it. Read it 10 or 20 times if necessary.

BE Yes. That is what I do, but it seems most others do not. They miss the logic of why TPS was created to begin with. As a result, they strive to establish TPS when it may not be necessary, or they don't understand why TPS is necessary. I realize this seems a trivial point to you, but most people have failed to grasp it. Managers pursue TPS as if it were a mere add-on to existing management practices. They cannot follow the logic, so I'd like to talk about it here in some detail.

TO I see. Prior to the World War II, the automobile market was controlled by the Government. It was a sellers' market. After the War, the automobile market was deregulated. Customers gained control of the market. Management can either fight the free market and risk survival of the company, or it can respond to the free market in ways that strengthen the competitiveness of the company. We chose to strengthen our competitiveness by creating a production system that could flexibly respond to the new buyers' markets that we faced. Other automakers chose to maintain their existing production system and change other things in the hope of responding adequately to the new buyers' market in Japan.

BE What was the logic for creating TPS?

TO The existence of buyers' markets meant that we had no choice but to produce a variety of products in small quantities in order to satisfy individual requirements under conditions of low demand. There is no way to do this affordably using the traditional batch-and-queue production method. The company would quickly go bankrupt. So, our challenge in manufacturing was to find low cost methods to produce small quantities tailored to meet individual needs. Because we did not have the answer to begin with, we had to experiment constantly to find new methods to produce small numbers of items at low cost. We took ideas from various sources, built upon other ideas, and added many new ideas of our own. Kaizen was the method we used for experimentation. Kaizen itself was developed and improved over time as the means by which we pursued cost reduction. That was our response to buyers' markets, and it resulted in customer satisfaction, growth, profitability, and survival. Over time, customers increasingly realized their power in the marketplace, for satisfaction of individual requirements, and so TPS evolved steadily in response to that. That is why I say, any business that sells into competitive markets can benefit from TPS.

BE It seems that companies that operate in sellers' markets would have no need for TPS.

TO That is true. Management is better off pursuing other things. However, one must always remember that times change, and so sellers' markets do not last forever. Therefore, managers who reap the rewards of sellers' markets become complacent and are doomed when the shift to buyers' markets eventually comes.

BE They are doomed because they do not know how to compete.

TO Correct! Having a sellers' market means that management can take it easy and still make a lot of money, whether customers are happy or not. But, sooner or later, customers will become unhappy and the market will change. Management, having been complacent for decades, suddenly has to compete for customers, and they do not know how to do it. Imagine if I sit around all day and did no exercise for many years, while you run 5 kilometers every day for many years. Then, the day comes when I am required to run against you in a competition. I am non-competitive and quickly fall behind. Managers in this bad situation will give serious consideration to taking shortcuts or cheating in order to improve their competitiveness and survive. Complacency seems cheap, but it is expensive and can be ruinous.

BE Given the crisis they face, management's typical response to ensure survival is to buy up their competitors and try to re-create sellers' markets to gain pricing power again.

TO And they may succeed. But, they still do not know how to compete. So more years of complacency set in, until the time comes when they once again face a buyers' market. This is why I say that any business must know how to compete, because is necessary now or will be necessary sometime in the future. Knowing how to compete is fundamental and necessary for survival. For example, a pharmaceutical company with a patented drug can charge a high price. Customers may grumble, but they have no other choice. Then one day, the patent expires and the drug company loses 95 percent of their market share overnight due to low-priced generic drug company competition. Not knowing how to compete has cost them dearly. If the pharmaceutical company were adept at TPS, it could expand its profit margins while simultaneously lowering the price of the drug to customers and meeting any other needs they may have. The lower price positions the company to maintain a higher market share when the patent expires and they begin to face competition from generic pharmaceutical companies. Or, they could take market share from the generic companies by improving their processes. The point is, practicing TPS even in a sellers' market prepares the company for the eventuality of competition. By avoiding complacency, they avoid the shock of losing 95 percent of their market share overnight. Such a loss in market share is a disaster. I do not understand why it is not recognized as such.

BE Business, unlike sports, is unusual in that there are mechanisms in place, such as patents, that permit or even encourage management complacency.

TO To that I simply say, beware. Managers will take any opportunity that allows them to relax and avoid competition. This cannot be allowed. Customers must not be exposed to such shabby treatment. They will remember how they were treated and someday strike back.

BE Many people today think TPS does not apply to their company because Toyota produces millions of automobiles, while they produce far fewer or different items.

TO That is a stupid way to think. Toyota, for many years, was a small startup company struggling to survive. Just go look at our production figures in the late-1940s, 1950s, and 1960s. We developed TPS during that period, and through the 1970s, while we were still small in terms of overall output. TPS has continued to evolve as times change. TPS was created under conditions similar to many small companies. The utility or success of TPS is unrelated to the size of the company or the type of company. When people say TPS does not apply to their company, it is an excuse to remain complacent and preserve their comfort. Managers who say this owe the company money and should return their paycheck.

BE To summarize, Most companies serve buyers markets. Therefore, companies must be managed in a way that is responsive to the marketplace it faces. TPS is a management system for competitive buyers' markets.

TO Yes. However, many companies serve both sellers' and buyers' markets. But this does not matter. The main idea is to learn how to compete. Even if it is not required presently, it will surely be required in the future. Management must assure that the company is positioned to thrive in the future no matter what the circumstances. Kaizen is fundamental for achieving this. However, kaizen is not the only method we use to identify and correct abnormalities. Late, outdated, or inaccurate information – human or computer – is a feature of the sellers' market batch-and-queue production system. This poor quality information cannot exist in TPS because it is demand-driven. Therefore, information must be both current and accurate, particularly information coming from the marketplace. TPS is a system for rapidly responding to current marketplace information; the demand from buyers' markets. Kaizen help assure information is both current and accurate, and that such information can be processed quickly in order to satisfy the unique needs of individual customers.

In What Ways Did This Conversation Improve Your Understanding of TPS?

-

-

-

-

How Will This Reduce Your Struggles?

-

-

-

-

Kaizen

BE In your book *Toyota Production System*, you never say "kaizen." You say "rationalization" and "improvement." Are these the same as kaizen? Seeing as how kaizen is fundamental to TPS, why did you not refer to it directly?

TO At the time I wrote the book in 1978, I had some interest in not revealing too many details of our methods. The book was intended for managers, not engineers trying to implement TPS. And so my focus was more on the concepts and mindset. I did not fully disclose these things because they were our true source of competitive advantage. The term "rationalization" differs depending on context. It can mean kaizen, but not usually. In *Toyota Production System*, I frequently said "improvement," often in the context of improving efficiency. "Improvement" is an accurate English interpretation for the Japanese word "kaizen." In *Workplace Management*, I refer to kaizen as "improvement" and "operational improvement." I provided other information that revealed the importance of observation, understanding the details of how work is performed, and waste, unevenness, and unreasonableness. There was a section in the book titled "Advocating Profit-Making Industrial Engineering." So if one recognizes the importance of industrial engineering (IE) to understanding the work, then with some imagination and creativity, anyone can find the path for turning IE into a profit-making activity for the company. This way, operations contributes to profit instead of merely existing as a cost, which is how accountants understand operations. To make progress, one has to carefully observe the work and try things out. One without the other is useless.

BE Unfortunately, the discipline of industrial engineering began to decline in America in the early 1990s in both university and in industry. And it continues to this day. Company leaders do not understand IE and do not consider it to be important.

TO That is their loss. They are destined to expend their precious resources processing waste, unevenness, and unreasonableness, rather than meeting individual customer's needs. The trouble is that spending all day processing waste, unevenness, and unreasonableness puts the company at risk for failure and will harm employees and suppliers. It is irresponsible of leaders to not understand the details of how work is performed. This is a basic or fundamental part of TPS. So this must interest you?

BE Yes, is of great interest to me. Some engineers from Toyota group companies left their employers in the late 1980s and, at your behest, began to teach TPS in America, Europe, and elsewhere. They taught "JIT/TPS" and kaizen. It seems to me that "JIT" was in line with how Americans and others understood TPS at that time; that TPS is JIT. The "JIT/TPS" training course offering was market-driven and therefore would attract an audience.

TO Perhaps so. People had an easier time understanding the concept of Just-in-Time, and mistakenly assumed it was the same as TPS, which was more difficult for them to understand. We tried for many years to correct this.

BE After a few years, the engineers' focus shifted from teaching JIT/TPS to teaching Toyota's kaizen method almost exclusively.

TO Yes. That is because it is difficult to teach TPS. The mindset is different and the methods are different. It is easier to teach people kaizen, which will lead them to TPS if they practice kaizen continuously. Toyota kaizen develops a new mindset and generates many ideas for new methods. For example, understanding the work will result in many delays or queues becoming visible. It will soon become obvious that these must be eliminated. The need for flow will become self-evident. The means for achieving flow will be things like JIT, autonomation, standard work, kanban, poka-yoke, andon, and so on. They will discover these things themselves, or with a little help from me or others who have written about TPS or trained people in TPS.

BE So am I correct to say that JIT cannot be established without kaizen? Nor can kanban or any other operational method? That kaizen is a fundamental for understanding work and how to improve work? That kaizen exposes waste, unevenness, and unreasonableness, and generates an awareness through hands-on experiences, which, over time, evolves into a new mindset through leaning.

TO That is more-or-less correct. I would simply say that kaizen is the basic method used to create TPS and how it has evolved in response to changing times. Without kaizen, TPS stagnates. Everything stops, so there is no TPS any longer. I would like to again state that Toyota's kaizen method is based on industrial engineering, but modified in many ways, both in thinking and practice, so that it results in profit improvement through cost reduction. IE that does not reduce costs and increase profits is useless.

BE Then, it is true to say that Toyota-style IE is a unique form of IE upon which TPS is based? In other words, there is no TPS without Toyota-style IE. And Toyota-style IE is the basis for kaizen.

TO Yes. I want to add that kaizen can never be learned in school or in a classroom. It can only be learned at the genba, by doing, not by watching.

BE It seems that many ideas for improvement come from conference rooms and brainstorming. The result is that employees make improvement that are easy for them to make, not improvements that are difficult to make, which are necessary to make, and which will help the company survive. They avoid challenges.

TO That's no good. What is the company paying employees for if all they do is work on easy things? Making improvements makes people feel good. But if the improvement results from human intelligence and ingenuity, and contributes to cost reduction and survival, then people will feel even better. This will motivate them to think harder about new improvements that contribute to cost reduction and survival. This is what all employees are being paid for, including managers.

BE What do we make of managers whose contributions increase costs and threaten survival?

TO That's no good. Because they are not helping the company, they should fire themselves.

BE The stopwatch, which is a fundamental tool in time and motion studies, is necessary for understanding work and making waste visible. But the stopwatch has a bad reputation. People believe operational improvement can be made without knowing cycle times and task times.

TO This is because the stopwatch has been used incorrectly. At Toyota, we use observation and the stopwatch to understand and improve work; to simplify work and better utilize available resources. It is not used to speed people up or make their work more difficult. Without the stopwatch, it is not possible to synchronize work and improve flow. The outcome we seek is customer satisfaction by meeting individual needs. The only way to do this without going bankrupt is one-piece flow.

BE In conducting time and motion studies with a stopwatch, I could see things that I had never seen before. This, in turn, gave me many ideas for improving the work.

TO The stopwatch is to an engineer what a compass is to a pilot. It tells you the direction of improvement. The basics of kaizen include the standard production capacity sheet, standard work sheet, standard work combination sheet, time observation form, yamazumi chart, and so on. The actual work performed is unknown until such details are thoroughly understood. Only then can it be improved. People are fooling themselves if they think work can be improved in the absence of understanding these details.

There may be some small gains, but cost reduction and increased profit will not be forthcoming.

BE This raises an interesting point. Many companies try to copy TPS, usually using a lesser interpretation or derivative, and then, after much effort, find little or no positive business results. Management then becomes frustrated that their investments have yielded less than they had hoped for.

TO Concepts related to TPS are easy to for people to understand, but the details are difficult to understand. One cannot establish TPS based on concepts alone. The work performed must be thoroughly understood. The people who actually do the production work are usually so busy doing the work that they cannot step back and understand their work in detail. They provide many improvement ideas, but others have to help by observing the work, conducting time and motion studies, making improvements, observing the effect of improvement on the work and the worker, making additional changes, and so on. This collaboration between people, to understand the work in detail, is the source of business results. It is foolish to think that business results will be achieved in the absence of Toyota-style IE. The variants of TPS, which I know nothing about, may be missing this and other necessary elements. TPS is like golf in that never-ending daily practice is needed on the golf course – the genba – by trying many things in many different ways, forever, because things change constantly. This is how results are achieved every daily. Many managers think it is good enough to achieve results periodically. At Toyota, we work to achieve results on a daily basis by paying close attention to the actual work being performed in relation to actual marketplace needs.

BE Not only are business results meager, but it takes a long time for them to achieve meager results.

TO Companies that operate in competitive markets do not have the luxury of taking a long time to achieve results. They are lethargic and will not survive. This is management's fault.

BE Their progress is even slower than you imagine because most companies use project management methods for their improvement activities.

TO This is completely wrong. Kaizen must occur so quickly that it takes less time to improve than it takes to define a project. I don't know where people get such ideas.

BE I believe it is because people indiscriminately apply the tools they learned in the past to any new task or challenge that they are faced with. In this case, kaizen.

TO This is an example of what I mean by abandoning preconceptions. Project management is the preconception that must be abandoned for kaizen to be effective.

BE It is also common for people to change the kaizen method in other ways that weaken it. Kaizen is diluted to people's present level of capabilities, to gain acceptance.

TO That must never happen. It will only result in the appearance of improvement. People's level of capabilities must be brought up by kaizen. Your process is your workshop. Improve yourself and your process.

In What Ways Did This Conversation Improve Your Understanding of TPS?

-
-
-
-

How Will This Reduce Your Struggles?

-
-
-
-

Speed of Improvement

BE May we talk about the speed of improvement? By that I mean the pace at which improvements are tried or made. I don't think this comes across clearly in your books.

TO Yes. This is a good topic.

BE It seems to me that for Toyota to advance from near bankruptcy to becoming a global force in the automotive industry within about 30 years, the pace of improvement must have been very rapid – rapid in a way that others cannot easily image.

TO That is likely so. Given that our chances for survival were dim after the War, we had to develop a mindset that there might be no tomorrow. We could not improve quickly by having meetings in conference rooms. By positioning ourselves on the genba, we were able to come up with new ideas many times a day and immediately try them out. That was the only way to know if our ideas would work. It was mostly trial-and-error. Many times we did not think the ideas would work. But I asked people to stop thinking and instead try out every idea that they had with their own hands – even if they thought the idea had no chance of working. Try it, and eliminate it quickly from consideration. But make sure you try it. From that we learned what worked and what did not work, much better than by thinking alone. It is surprising that thinking can both help and hinder progress. Most people believe that thinking always helps matters progress. Thinking can often be a hindrance. That is why I say, "Stop thinking; just try it" or "Do it, then think."

Use your intelligence to do it, then use your intelligence to think. This is another true source of competitive advantage that I did not discuss in detail. I alluded to it on occassion.

BE So TPS could never have been designed by thinking and planning the system, and then implementing it in a systematic fashion.

TO Never. Perhaps today, now that more is known about TPS, someone will outline some basic steps to be taken and which methods are necessary and can be re-used. But even with a practical framework and established methods, there remains much trial-and-error and experimentation. Kaizen never goes away, even if many exact steps are given.

BE I know it is impossible to put numbers to it, but if a typical company makes changes at a rate of 1, would Toyota be 10?

TO More like 100 or 1000. Numbers, however, can deceive. But, what does not deceive is reality. So you must react quickly to reality as it changes. The number does not matter. Taking action quickly is what matters. Be lightning-quick.

BE What drove that pace of change?

TO A determination to survive. Cherry blossoms have great symbolism in Japanese culture. The symbolism includes living in the present, change, impermanence, transience, renewal, beauty, optimism, celebration, life, and death. If you observe a cherry tree, it looks a little different every day of its blooming cycle. Likewise, the genba will look a little different every day because small improvements are made every day in response to abnormal conditions. Cherry blossoms last only about a week. No improvement should last more than about a week. If that happens, then it is obvious that people have stopped thinking. We were able to survive because employees kept thinking and made changes every day. That is how Toyota continues to survive.

BE Many managers from other companies would say that Toyota's leaders no longer have to be concerned about survival.

TO That is the mindset that leads to a company's decline and perhaps its ultimate failure. It is wrong to think that way. It is like a baseball team with a big lead that becomes complacent and loses the game. Whether you are ahead or behind, managers must never be complacent.

BE Perhaps that mindset is why companies make improvements so slowly and are unable to establish TPS even after 10 or 20 years. Today, most leaders seem to think that survival is automatic. They appear to be less interested in survival of the company and more interested in when they can sell the company at a high price and personally and profit from the sale, whether the company is in good shape or not. In fact, some leaders make more money when the company is in bankruptcy than before.

TO This is a strange view of executive responsibility.

BE It is a view of responsibility to shareholders.

TO And what of the other stakeholders? They have responsibilities to them as well.

BE Yes, but they don't seem to care much about them.

TO TPS cannot be established under such idiotic conditions. Any improvements will soon be undone. Managers who try may see some positive results, or the illusion of positive results. Subordinates can be very good at tricking their boss into thinking that improvement has been achieved. They have their own survival in mind.

BE Returning to the pace of change, how did you establish or promote that beyond the need for survival.

TO It is well known that I gave people challenging tasks and told them I would return to see what they had done. I did not say when I would return, so that put pressure on them to try out their ideas quickly. Another ingredient was my demeanor. As I said in my books, I had to go crazy in order to advance my way of thinking and establish TPS. By crazy, I mean it in the sense of describing a strong determination. I was very hard on people; I pushed them as far as I could and certainly further than they wanted. It was difficult for everyone involved. Upon reflection, I believe most would say that, given the times and the needs, it was appropriate. Times have changed. I am sure that other methods can be used to motivate people to embrace a rapid pace of change.

BE Isn't it true that one of the benefits that employees see from Toyota-style kaizen is rapid improvement, which is uplifting? Without kaizen, there is perpetual stagnation, which is demoralizing. The usual pace of improvement in the absence of kaizen is so slow that it drains human energy and enthusiasm.

TO Yes. People who have been given a challenge and see that they are able to do what they never thought they could do leaves them energetic and striving for more. Making things better is good medicine for the mind and body, and for the company. But is no good if improvement happens slowly. Improvement must happen quickly, every day, many times a day, by everyone, at all levels, because everyone experiences abnormalities every day. There is no exception. The speed at which we learned how to improve operations was very useful to Toyota overall for learning how adapt to changing market conditions. We had to be quick when I was in charge. But times have changed. Today, you have to be lightning-quick.

BE It is well known that bureaucracy disables people's imagination and interest in engaging in trial-and-error and experimentation.

TO At Toyota, we have many strict rules, procedures, and policies. But management assures that this does not stand in the way of people generating ideas for improvement and trying them out on a daily basis. If bureaucracy cripples the company's ability to adapt to changing conditions, then I think management is irresponsible and they will doom the company.

BE The way most companies adapt is by buying other companies or product lines.

TO They need to learn to adapt within themselves, without the need to resort to expensive and disruptive actions such as mergers and acquisitions. Such activities must be the exception, not the rule. Managers must lead the way, as the need for adaptability continues to grow now and into the future. Becoming more bureaucratic is the opposite of what is needed in these rapidly changing times.

BE Teamwork must be different than how most people understand it when improvement occurs at a rapid pace. Can you comment on that?

TO People must work together as a team to achieve results. But, it is possible to work well together as a team and achieve nothing. What good is that? Teamwork must be driven by actual needs with clear improvement targets in mind. Every business has a need for two things: cost reduction and survival. Teamwork must respond to these two needs, as well as targets that have been identified. This applies to both routine work and kaizen. This helps drive the rapid pace of improvement. Success diminishes the perceived need to remain focused on cost reduction and survival. People today may feel more comfortable and no longer understand the meaning of teamwork in relation to these two fundamental needs. Teamwork is stronger when one is struggling to survive than it is when maintaining one's success. Under this condition, teamwork strongly promotes mutual cooperation.

In What Ways Did This Conversation Improve Your Understanding of TPS?

-
-
-
-

How Will This Reduce Your Struggles?

-
-
-
-

Cost Reduction

BE In your books, you emphasize the importance of cost reduction and profit improvement as an outcome of kaizen, Toyota-style industrial engineering, which is the basis of TPS. Cost reduction is widely interpreted among managers as the elimination of labor from the company...

TO Stop! This is a big misunderstanding. One result of kaizen may be the elimination of persons from a process, but it does not mean their elimination from the company. People who have been eliminated from a process are assigned to work in other areas that require additional labor. As all manager seek growth, there will be no trouble making use of the excess labor produced as a result of kaizen. Even if a company is in decline, it is up to managers to assure stable employment. They must sacrifice their own interests before employees' interests.

BE Why must managers assure stable employment?

TO Isn't it obvious? I do not know why I even have to say it! Eliminating persons from the company as a result of improvement halts the ability of employees to adapt to changing conditions. They do not utilize training; they do not think of new ideas; they do not try out their new ideas; and they do not learn. It is disaster. Improvement must always be accompanied with a good heart. They go together, to support people's efforts to improve their work. Heartlessness steals the desire from people to improve their work. Management must not be thieves.

BE In my experience, "cost reduction" in a typical production system means "unit cost reduction" and "budget cutting," while "cost reduction" in TPS means "total cost reduction." Is this correct?

TO Yes. Labor is only one type of misunderstanding of what cost reduction means in TPS. There are many more. To the typical manager, "cost reduction" means "unit cost reduction" of a part. In TPS, "cost reduction" means "total cost reduction" for the company, not solely unit cost reduction of an item produced. Total cost reduction can only be achieved by improving flow, not by simple budget cutting. When flow is achieved, defective parts are not made or passed along, therefore quality improves and costs go down. When flow is improved, lead-times are shortened, inventories are reduced, and costs go down. Lower-cost equipment is used because the management thinking that supports "economies of scale" is abandoned. Lower cost equipment costs less to maintain or repair, and fewer maintenance personnel are needed. There is also less equipment and less items such as cutting tools and coolant, therefore further lowering costs. The company has a smaller base of employees because flow throughout all production and assembly processes is less labor intensive. These are just a few examples. Making things one-at-a-time is the lowest total cost method of production. Nobody believes that by thinking about it or by doing simple calculations. And they throw thinking-based arguments and simple calculations to prove that one-piece flow is wrong. You have to create flow with your own two hands and then you will know the truth. You understand the innumerable contributions to total cost that are reduced by flow.

BE And many of those costs do not appear on a financial spreadsheet. Cost reduction consists of things that you can easily see and measure, as well as costs that you cannot easily see or measure.

TO That is correct. By understanding and improving the work performed on the genba, you begin to see costs that are not visible on the accountant's spreadsheet. This is why I say that numbers deceive people. And this is why managers must understand the work at the genba. It takes 10 years of kaizen practice to understand costs. Managers who focus on only what is visible and measurable miss 25 percent or more of costs. Because they do not understand costs, they simply cut budgets. There is no skill in cutting budgets. Any idiot can put a red line through some numbers and write new numbers next to the old numbers. Cutting a budget is no more difficult than cutting tofu. Practicing kaizen to reduce total costs is a skill that it worthy of one who possesses the title of "manager."

BE What one learns about costs in 10 years of kaizen includes additional things such as hiring, training, motion, floor space, taxes, energy consumption, spirit, challenge, creativity, innovation, learning, teamwork, evolution, and more.

TO That too is correct.

BE Today, many people claim that TPS or its variants should not focus on cost reduction. They say that the focus on cost reduction results in failure to establish TPS.

TO That is nonsense. As I have said repeatedly, it is meaningless if Toyota-style IE does not result in cost reduction and profit increases. If this is not their interest, then they are free to define things as they wish. They will also likely define failure as success.

BE They say the focus should be on eliminating waste and increasing value, not cost reduction.

TO What is the difference? I think these are senseless arguments. TPS works. Do these other things work?

BE It depends. The closer they are to TPS, the better it works.

TO People must return to the two things that every business needs: 1) cost reduction and 2) survival. If they do not pursue these in a constructive way, then it is their loss.

BE This is part of the problem.

TO Not "problem." Abnormal condition.

BE This is part of the abnormal condition. Management does not pursue TPS in a constructive way. They pursue it in a destructive way.

TO How can one expect good results if TPS is pursued in a destructive way? Only a fool could think that is possible. It seems there are many fools.

In What Ways Did This Conversation Improve Your Understanding of TPS?

-
-
-
-

How Will This Reduce Your Struggles?

-
-
-
-

Respect for Humanity

BE In the Preface to the *Toyota Production System*, you said the TPS core concepts were the elimination of waste and "respect for humanity." The concept, "respect for humanity," is not typically associated with business. What did you mean by "respect for humanity?" Why is it, as you say, "equally important," to the elimination of waste?

TO Sakichi Toyoda's life and work as an inventor taught us many things, including the concept of "respect for humanity." This concept has multiple meanings. To begin, it means to make good use of your life as a human. How do you do that? It begins with taking personal responsibility and developing one's self. That is done by tirelessly pursuing one's interests. However, following one's interests can be done narrowly and selfishly. Or, it can be done in relation to a larger system or objective, such as serving the needs of a community or society-at-large. In this sense, the ultimate value of one's work is its contribution to society. Sakichi Toyoda's work contributed to Japanese society and beyond.

BE One person can make great contributions to society, but not everyone is so fortunate.

TO That is true. Yet every individual is capable of taking personal responsibility and developing themselves in relation to their work. By developing one's self in relation to their work – meaning, by improving their own work through study and trial-and-error – they will perform the work better and provide good results to subsequent workers. In this way, they respect humans with whom they work, whether they reside inside the company or not. People make valuable contributions that, individually may have no visible impact on society. But collectively, whether as individuals or teams, they have a great impact on society.

BE So everyone, in their own unique way, and to the extent that they can, develops their capabilities in the work that they do. Whether as individuals or teams, they are responsive to the concept of "respect for humanity."

TO Yes, provided that they have a willingness, sustained over many years, to improve. It has little to do with talent. Effort is what matters. With effort comes imagination, which generates many new ideas to try, and progress is made today and for tomorrow. This is how to keep up with the times. Keeping up with the times, or not falling behind, respects humanity.

BE "Respect for humanity" suggests one should strive to harmonize business with nature, of which humanity is a part of.

TO That is correct. One way to do that is to make what is needed, when it is needed, in the amount needed. In other words, to consume no more resources that is actually necessary to satisfy individual customer demand. Why produce more than is needed? Humanity will have difficulty surviving if it depletes its own resources. This is why I say TPS has great value not just to business, but to humanity, and why 30 years ago I asked my subordinates to go out into the world and teach the basics of TPS to others.

BE "Respect for humanity" has meanings that span many levels. In 2001, Toyota produced an internal document called "The Toyota Way 2001." The English version identified "Continuous Improvement" and "Respect for People" as the pillars of The Toyota Way. I find it curious that it was not translated as "Kaizen" and "Respect for Humanity." Are the meanings the same?

TO As is almost always the case, the meaning in Japanese is different than the interpretations in English. For example, "kaizen" means "improvement." Adding the word "continuous" clarifies the intent, which is for improvement to be endlessly repeated because there is no end to improvement. "Continuous Improvement" does not mean solely to continuously improve work processes or product. It also means to continuously improve one's self; it means the development of subordinates by superiors; and it means the development of suppliers by parent companies. "Respect for Humanity" carries a broader sense then "Respect for People," but both must exist. Yet neither term completely captures or expresses the concept. This is complicated and more difficult to explain than other things we have talked about. Let me simply say this: The core concepts of TPS, and what is now known as the pillars of The Toyota Way, reflect timeless values of our founders and things that we learned, through trial-and-error, in creating TPS. If humanity is not respected, then one's work detracts from society instead of contributing to it. Discord flourishes instead of harmony, and nature is thrown out of balance. When things are out of balance, results can look good – such as numbers in a report – but the actual condition of the company and its people is very bad. Waste flourishes when things are out of balance.

BE So one must think broadly about the meanings that the two TPS concepts, now known as pillars of The Toyota Way, convey. Such broad-mindedness seems rare, as managers readily accept discord and imbalances. For example, they view the elimination of waste merely as a means of achieving unit cost savings and cannot comprehend how that outcome is related to "Respect for Humanity" – or they simply don't care. In organizations that follow American-style business thinking, unit cost savings causes disrespect to humanity. People suffer job loss in management's drive to reduce unit costs and increase profits. Suppliers are forced to reduce prices to the point where they make no profit or suffer losses. These commonly occur in companies that try to establish TPS.

TO Earlier I said that concepts related to TPS are easy to for people to understand, but the details are difficult to understand. In this case, both the concepts and the details are difficult to understand. The only way "Kaizen" and "Respect for humanity" can become understandable is when one gains experience by trying things. For example, by trying things one learns that the lowest total cost is achieved when things are in balance – flow. Eliminating waste improves balance, as well as harmony. The only way to learn this is by doing. Though, I have observed that sometimes leading is not learning. The two can be separated for one's own convenience.

BE What do you mean by that?

TO Learning is fundamental to advancing in the management ranks, from worker to line supervisor to unit manager and so on. Leading and learning are connected to one another. However, once people advance to the topmost positions, they seem to separate leading from learning. They focus on leading and largely abandon learning. Achieving high position is something like a student graduating from university, where receiving a diploma can suggest to some people they now know things thoroughly and are done with their studies. For this reason, training senior leaders is a very difficult undertaking. I think everyone know this. A company's leaders might say they want TPS, but do they possess the will to learn as well as the will to lead? If leading has been decoupled from learning, then efforts to establish TPS will soon fail. That is why at Toyota management training occurs at the genba, because evidence of learning is indisputable. Top managers can easily fool others to think that they have learned something when training takes place only in the classroom. If there are 20 things to learn in genba kaizen, and 20 things to learn in classroom training, top managers will have learned 40 things in genba kaizen and two things from the classroom training. And, of the two things learned in the classroom, one will be useless. This is why I say that true leadership can only be learned at the genba. Leading and learning must not be decoupled.

BE It is widely known that you were very difficult or harsh; that you behaved badly towards people, whether they reported to you or not. So I hear people say: "What are we to make of Ohno-san who says 'respect humanity' but he was very disrespectful. People feared him." Or, they say, "A pillar of The Toyota Way is 'Respect for People.' Ohno-san was rough with people, not respectful." What do you say to this criticism?

TO It is true that I was not easy on people. I encountered much resistance and had many fights with people. I was not well liked by some people, perhaps more than I know. But I have no interest in justifying my behaviors. Times today are different than the times I worked in. The attitudes, values, and needs of individuals and society are different. This should be obvious. People often say that if they had to do it over again, they would do it differently. However, time flows only in one direction, so saying one would do things differently is an empty gesture. There is no going back. Because time flows only in one direction, we have the opportunity for evolution, if such opportunity is taken. My disciples took my teachings and evolved them, just as I asked. Some did so better than others. One must also understand that "Respect for Humanity" or "Respect for People" are not knowable concepts, nor are they static in time. "Respect for Humanity" or "Respect for People" cannot be fully grasped at the outset of one's effort to establish TPS – even though much more is known about TPS today. You start with a concept and develop your understanding of it over time in relation to an objective. The two co-evolve. Our desire was to create a uniquely Japanese production system responsive to the buyers' market we faced. In addition, there are many ways to express "Respect for Humanity" or "Respect for People." One's ability to do so advances with practice. They become more deft. Focusing on my past behaviors ignores how the concept of "Respect for Humanity" has evolved in TPS at Toyota. Evolution is a natural consequence of the continuation of kaizen by successive generations.

BE I would like to connect your thoughts about leading and learning to what you said about "Respect for Humanity" or "Respect for People" as not being knowable concepts.

TO TPS is merely a name given to the way Toyota makes things. But because the way Toyota makes things is ever-changing, TPS itself is not knowable. Therefore, no concept or method of TPS is completely knowable. Enshrining TPS knowledge as words or pictures on the pages of books do not make it knowable. This is a deception. Knowing is the product of one's practice over time. It reflects an evolution in thinking and methods. If thinking stops and methods remain fixed, then evolution has stopped and knowing becomes frozen in time. Leading and learning become decoupled when one thinks they know things. They think they have arrived at a point in their career where doing things is all that matters. They have given up and allowed themselves to become frozen in time. This must never happen to leaders because they are responsible for the lives of many other people.

BE Many people claim to be experts in TPS, which suggests an attainment of complete knowing has been achieved.

TO Experts are frozen in time. People disrespect themselves and others when they call themselves "expert." Expertise is fixed. Improvement is infinite. Trouble arises when one relies on those who are frozen in time, expert or not.

BE We often say that the person who does the work is the expert. Are workers frozen in time?

TO Yes, insofar as their focus on doing the job means that they cannot observe their own work. Of course any worker can come up with ideas for improvement, but, strictly speaking, they cannot observe themselves doing their work – unless they record it and watch it later. The distinction is not one of expertise; meaning, who is the expert or who is not. This is where I think people get confused. The distinction is working in isolation versus working in teams. Working alone can lead the mindless repetition of tasks with few ideas and little incentive to improve. The human interaction associated with teamwork results in conversations about the work that lead to concrete actions for improvement. For example, a worker may not notice idleness, but someone observing the worker will. The two can discuss the idle time and discover why it is occurring and generate ideas together to eliminate it.

BE What are your thoughts on "Respect for Humanity" as companies pursue digital strategies?

TO They must be consistent with one another. The replacement of physical processes with computer-based processes does not eliminate the concept of "Respect for Humanity." In fact, the opposite is true. Transitioning to more computer-based processes requires greater attention to the concept of "Respect for Humanity." There is a danger that in the fervent effort to computerize processes, in the hope of realizing all of its promises, that its effects on humans will be neglected in various ways.

In What Ways Did This Conversation Improve Your Understanding of TPS?

-
-
-
-

How Will This Reduce Your Struggles?

-
-
-
-

Day Two
Conversation

Japanese Language

BE People criticize the use of Japanese language or terms used in TPS training. They substitute different words for the Japanese words. What do you have to say about that?

TO In *Toyota Production System*, I spoke about Japanese language using tōfu as an example. The example may have been too abstract and people missed the point. I was seeking to communicate the way Japanese language influences how we think. TPS is the result of how we think about things. Therefore, TPS and the Japanese language are intimately related.

BE So it reflects a thought process?

TO Yes. The thought process and how information is interpreted. This, in turn, reflects the imagination, creativity, and innovations that go into TPS. The Japanese language was therefore important in the development of TPS. It still is, as TPS evolves at Toyota.

BE Can you give another example?

TO Jidoka, ji • do • ka, means "autonomation;" automation with a human touch. It means to give the machine human intelligence so that it stops automatically when an abnormal condition occurs. The kanji character for "do" contains a symbol that represents people. It means "do by people." Therefore, human intelligence is given to the automated machine. The kanji characters for "do" in the word "automation" does not contain a symbol for people. This is an example of how we think, which is embedded throughout TPS.

BE So, in order to understand TPS, it is helpful to understand how the Japanese language influenced the thinking as it relates to creativity and innovation, and to achieve the normal condition, flow.

TO Yes, that is correct. I do not think TPS, as I knew it up until my retirement from Toyota, could have been created in any language that uses the Roman alphabet. It does not contain the pictorial or graphical richness to spark creativity or convey ideas in the way that Japanese characters do.

BE This is another reason why it is difficult for non-Japanese speaking people to understand TPS.

TO Japanese people have difficulty with TPS as well. They understand the language, but TPS is a different way of thinking.

BE So if someone wants to learn TPS, they should put some effort into to understanding things more deeply. One needs a strong very strong and long-lasting will to learn.

TO This is true. But even Japanese people need someone experienced in TPS to help explain things. Otherwise, it does not make sense.

BE What other Japanese elements or factors are important?

TO TPS draws on of facets unique to Japan and Japanese life. In addition to language, we think in terms of Japanese daily living, Shinto and Buddhism, Japanese history and traditions. It was part of my desire to create a uniquely Japanese production technology, in response to the conditions that we faced. These factors were important contributors to achieving that outcome.

BE This is what some people find so interesting, and what others find so difficult or unnecessary.

TO I see. Those who wish to de-couple Japanese language and thinking from TPS should stop complaining about it and work diligently. They must practice kaizen intensely.

BE Many people don't like the word "kaizen." They say "rapid improvement workshop," "improvement event," "CI project," or thigs similar to that.

TO At some point, the use of different words results in the loss of all meaning. It leads to a different way of thinking than ours. I hope they do not expect TPS outcomes if their understanding and practice is totally different.

BE That is indeed what they expect.

TO Then they are mad to think that it is possible.

BE What if the thinking is different, but the methods practiced are the same or close to what is practiced in TPS?

TO I believe the two go together; the thinking and the practice cannot be different. The practice without the thinking will lead to different results. Maybe the different or limited results they achieve meet their needs. It is up to them to judge if that is so, not me. I can only speak about TPS, not the many ways other people might understand it or practice it.

BE This is why some people use consultants experienced in TPS. They get closer to TPS than the others.

TO I would expect that result if the client carefully follows the consultant's guidance. TPS is difficult but worthwhile. It strengthens a company's competitiveness through the development of human capabilities. The difficulty is that it is transmitted most effectively from one experienced person to another person with less experience.

BE People then complain about the time it takes to learn TPS.

TO People spend too much time complaining. Rather than complain, they should be curious and learn how our way of thinking led to new ways of doing things. They should just do it. You cannot establish TPS by complaining. You have to make TPS with your own two hands by trial-and-error. You have to try many ideas and make many mistakes quickly, and improve lightning-quick. People think they know how to make a wooden table. They don't know how to make it until they have made one. They don't know how to make a good wooden table until they have made 100. It is better made after making it 1000 times. Of course, a carpenter who does this thinks about their work and their product, and discovers ways of improving both. If a carpenter makes the table exactly same way 1000 times, then there no learning beyond the establishment of basic skills after they make 20 or 30 tables.

BE It is obvious that learning is a foundational part of TPS.

TO While that is true, there are things that must precede learning. Otherwise, you can learn by simply reading words on a page. Learning begins with observation of the work and discovering abnormal conditions, such as stagnation, backflows, and so on, followed by thinking of ways to return to the normal condition. Nobody can pre-determine which ideas will work. This is like predicting the future; it cannot be done. We have preconceived notions of what might work better, but we do not know with certainty. We might guess correctly, but then learning will be limited to the one idea that was tried. Therefore, all ideas must be tried.

BE Getting people to try things is difficult. Organizations are hierarchical, and hierarches to undercut people's interest in trying things. They fear being blamed if something goes wrong. They seek approvals before trying things. If approvals take a long time to get, then the amount of trying slows down and people eventually stop trying.

TO Management is responsible for this abnormal condition. People follow rules, whether they are written or not. If the rules discourage trying things or experimenting, then management must identify the root causes and apply countermeasures. People follow their habits. If they have 20 years of practice brainstorming, then this habit must be broken at once and replaced with a new habit of trystorming. Both management and employees must work together, and each must develop new habits. This is the essence of TPS.

BE What other abnormal conditions is management responsible for?

TO Anything that prevents material and information flow, in production or in any other process. All companies produce. And each one has a system of production, whether the managers recognize it or not. There is a connected network of processes within production, external to production but within the company, and external to the company. It is all connected. All parts of the network of connected processes will experience abnormal conditions. Management is responsible for all of it. As the severity of the abnormality increases, then successively higher levels of management must become involved quickly. Their role is to understand the abnormality and help return to the normal condition. Managers must not blame workers for the occurrence of abnormal conditions, because doing so will prevent material and information flow. Instead, the first words managers must say to workers is: "Thank you for bringing this to my attention." This way of thinking comes from Japanese daily living.

In What Ways Did This Conversation Improve Your Understanding of TPS?

-

-

-

-

How Will This Reduce Your Struggles?

-

-

-

-

Learn from Nature

BE In kaizen, we are asked to think about nature and observe how nature solves problems. At first, this seems impossible because we do not think this way. We assume nature takes care of nature's problems and that businesspeople take care of our business problems. The two do not cross.

TO The basic idea is to learn from others. In doing so, one has two choices. Learn from others who do things poorly or from those who do things well. The distinction pertains to qualities such as simplicity, efficiency, effectiveness, minimum consumption of resources, and so on. To copy methods that produce waste, unevenness, and unreasonableness is stupid and increases risk to the company. Therefore, it is wise to learn from examples that reduce risk to the company. In many cases, this means reducing costs, but also safety, speed, and so on. But one must never blindly copy. Instead, one must understand the learning in relation to the improvement they seek to achieve. There is necessary back-and-forth that helps deepen one's understanding.

BE It is remarkable that today, still, people happily copy methods that produce waste, unevenness, and unreasonableness. We see what is around us without seeing. We follow others without thinking.

TO That is because they do not know what the normal condition is. They believe the existence of myriad problems

– mostly the same problems repeating many times – is normal. In nature, it is very easy to see the normal condition and abnormal conditions. A bird flying level upside down or a flock of birds flying into a building is an abnormal condition. It is obviously so. There is no need to check with a bird scientist. What I taught people was to determine the normal condition so that any abnormal condition will be easily identified and immediately rectified, thus bringing the process back to the normal condition. In this way, we reduce myriad costs and help assure profit for the company. Managers who do not know the normal condition allow the company to suffer lost profits due to the existence of abnormal conditions. In many cases, abnormal conditions are built into automated processes or information systems. This must not be accepted.

BE Humans are part of nature, but we create structures separate from it, and much less efficient than nature.

TO They are separate because no thought has been given to aligning them or bringing them together. TPS strives to do things the way nature does things. I always say that flow is the normal condition. Stagnation, queues, delays, are abnormal conditions. Is stagnation a normal condition in nature? Think about the flows in nature. How many different types of flow are there? What problems do these different types of flow solve?

BE Nature's solutions to problems are elegant, but can be incredibly complicated when studied in detail. When you direct people to look to see how nature solves problems, are you asking them to look at the details?

TO No. Biological processes is too great a level of detail. People are very good at making things complex. The purpose of thinking about nature is to break free of complexity and simplify. Therefore, I want people to think at a higher level, to understand nature's solutions to problems, which have evolved over millions of years, to enable specific functions to be performed. For example, how does nature move air, water, or earth? How do animals cling to surfaces or navigate obstacles? How do plants or animals protect themselves against harm? How is buoyancy used? And, importantly, how many different ways to these functions appear in nature. This shows there are many solutions to the same or similar problems in nature. Likewise, there are many countermeasures to address abnormal conditions in processes.

BE Using nature changes the frame of reference for problem-solving. It removes people from their traditional sources of solutions: spend money, hire more people, buy new equipment, and so on.

TO Yes. TPS was created using human creativity, imagination, ingenuity, and wisdom. Thinking about nature helps promote this and is necessary to establish TPS and for TPS to evolve, just as nature evolves. Using nature to stimulate ideas leads to cost reduction and profit improvement because the countermeasures to abnormal conditions are much simpler and less expensive.

BE Many thousands of people have toured Toyota facilities over 40 years. Why have they not seen these things and made them common management practice?

TO People see things without seeing. This is why I stress the importance of observation. When you go for a walk in the country, what do you see? Most likely you see only a rough outline of nature. And you are easily distracted by various things: a mosquito flying into your ear; a conversation, an airplane flying overhead, the cold or the heat, tired feet, your safety, your hunger or thirst, and so on. So while you may enjoy your walk in the country, there is probably little that you actually observe. This is why I say that countermeasures for abnormalities can be found by going for a walk in the country. The countermeasures are there, but they are invisible until you learn to see them. Learning from nature is a timeless challenge. There is no limit to what can be learned from nature.

BE Going for a walk in the workplace is the same as going for a walk in the country in that people do not notice things – normal or abnormal conditions.

TO This is why kaizen is so important: It teaches people how to notice normal or abnormal conditions, and how to quickly bring abnormal conditions back to normal. Managers must be trained in kaizen so that they can distinguish between normal and abnormal conditions when they walk around the workplace. This is a fundamental capability for a leader of TPS.

BE What if there is no workplace? What if people are working from home and are globally distributed?

TO It does not matter. People must find ways to distinguish between normal and abnormal under such conditions.

In What Ways Did This Conversation Improve Your Understanding of TPS?

-

-

-

-

How Will This Reduce Your Struggles?

-

-

-

-

Leading TPS

BE Why do you think you were successful in establishing TPS? Today, it is popular to talk about leadership and identify the secrets of leadership success so that others can copy them. There is a focus on leadership behaviors. People feared you. Is that still a necessary or useful behavior?

TO People who copy me do so at their own risk. I have no way of knowing if I am a good model or not for others to follow in these times. My behaviors were as they were then. There is no going back.

BE Evolution means behavior changes are necessary. Why do you think you were successful in establishing of TPS?

TO This being a different time suggests TPS must be established differently. Putting my behaviors aside, I did some things that may prove useful now and into the future. One's actions are a combination of the time-limited and the timeless. Some actions work in-time and other actions work for-time. It is difficult for me to judge which is which, but I shall try.

BE Thank you. I understand it is difficult to analyze one's own work and pick out certain useful things.

TO First, I always forced myself to think differently. Most people do not do this. They would rather take it easy, get along, and not make waves. But I could not see how to make progress if I thought the same way as everyone else. Again, I want to emphasize that I had to *force* myself to think differently, every day. This required the development of a personal disciple, but one which never becomes fully embedded because it is so easy to slip and begin think like everyone else. Second, I was determined to do what needed to be done to make progress. So we broke many rules for how work is supposed to be done. I did not think about rewards or punishment, commendation or condemnation. I had a sense of confidence that others felt and absorbed. When they achieved things they thought were impossible to achieve, their confidence grew, as did mine. So confidence-building worked in a reciprocal manner. This helped keep things going when times were tough. Third, I did not deliver great speeches. Managers' speeches have more to do with polishing one's ego than it does making progress. So instead, I spoke only briefly – enough to generate more questions for people to think about or ask. This had the effect of developing people's capabilities to think differently and quickly take action to try things. This is the essence of what I was trying to teach. So rather than saying I developed people, my true action was to provide limited feedback on their work so that they could develop themselves. Fourth, I was relentless in our pursuit of flow. We were committed and never deviated from our objectives. We were constant in our purpose over decades and believed that our efforts would contribute to the survival of the company. I was confident that the Japanese people had the capability to create a production system that met the needs of the times and that the world might someday admire. I have provided four insights into how I led the establishment of TPS. There are many other smaller details, but I think these were the main elements of my leadership. Now, it is critical to understand that I had total support from my superiors. I never had to ask permission to do the things I did. Company leaders learned the results of TPS and they never wavered in their support for it.

BE That is perhaps one of the most amazing things, that TPS continued to develop and evolve through generations of Toyota leaders. There has been a constancy of purpose. As a result, TPS has become widely admired. But the mindset and method that led to the creation of TPS is less admired. I believe it is because it is less understood. To me, the mindset and methods are most fascinating. I have been working to broaden people's understanding with the books I have written on kaizen, as well as this book. What else can you say about leading the establishment of TPS that you have not said elsewhere?

TO It seems many leaders prefer to do things their way rather than the way their customers want. There is always much talk among managers to do things for customers' benefit, but mostly they do things for themselves. This is complacency rooted in preconceptions. Modern business methods were developed more than 100 years ago in a time when companies could sell everything they made – a sellers' market. These methods still exist in businesses today, even though the marketplace is no longer the way it once was – buyers' markets are pervasive. Using sellers' market methods such as batch-and-queue processing for a buyers' market puts the company at a great disadvantage. To overcome this, they play money games. That cannot last. To regain competitiveness, post-modern business methods must be adopted throughout the company. They must abandon the batch-and-queue method and establish flow production. Top managers will become uncomfortable once they grasp the full meaning of flow: Everything changes. We all know that a single change must be led by someone. The establishment of flow requires change in every part of the company and in every process. This too must be led from the top. But because such changes happen over many years, all leaders must be engaged and fully committed. Top managers who are uncomfortable with the idea that everything must change are not the type of leaders that the company needs if it hopes to survive the competition.

BE Managers lose interest in TPS when they hear that change must happen over many years.

TO When I ask managers how long they intend to be around, they always say "many years." So if managers plan to be around for many years, they may as well make necessary changes to establish TPS.

BE As time has progressed, it is apparent that there is an even greater need to produce diverse items according to individual requirements under conditions of low demand.

TO That is true. Therefore, companies using methods developed 100 years ago are falling behind and in poor position to survive in the future. This is why small startup businesses are a threat to established businesses. They are not bound to 100-year old methods, and they recognize the need to produce diverse items according to individual requirements, and do so at lost cost and with quick delivery. Because established businesses have money, or, better to say they can obtain loans cheaply, they buy the startups that threaten them. Once it is acquired, the startup will either die or it will thrive. It is more likely to die as a sacrifice to its new owner who seeks to maintain its position in the marketplace and retain its archaic methods. Leaders who buy startups only to let them die are failures. These types of leaders are not needed. Individuals, companies, and societies regress under poor leadership of this type.

BE One reason that many business leaders are stuck in the past is due to business educational that still teaches 100-year old methods. Business schools have proven to be very influential, particularly over the last 40 years.

TO Anyone who does not question their education is a fool. Classroom education is good as far as it goes. But to become educated and then stop thinking makes no sense. Diplomas makes people overconfident in their knowledge. One diploma multiplies overconfidence by four times. Two diplomas multiply overconfidence by 16 times. Three diplomas multiply overconfidence by 256 times. That is why managers must learn the truth by participating in genba kaizen. They must lead with genba knowledge in mind, not with diploma knowledge in mind.

BE What do you make of professors who still teach 100-year old business methods?

TO It is obvious that business would benefit if professors taught post-modern business methods instead of modern business methods. Though, there is a basic question as to whether business methods can be taught without having had business experience. Can a person teach surgery if they have never performed surgery? Business education is odd in this way and must be reformed. Teaching old methods may be partly generational, but education systems typically lag what is happening in industry by many years. The objectives of each are different and they operate on different time scales. Some of these gaps must be narrowed. However, whatever the circumstance may be, it is up to the person with the diploma to continue learning. Those who stop learning must be removed from leadership positions because they are no longer capable of serving the interests of employees, customers, and others.

BE I find it odd that one can receive an advanced degree in business and not have ever taken a course in production systems. These people are then put in charge of production.

TO Many strange things happen in this world. People are free to do as they wish. But there are consequences. One hopes that in such cases, the person in charge of production would commit to personally studying production systems, particularly in relation to marketplace needs, and make necessary changes. When put into a leadership position, people must realize that their job is to lead. This seems obvious, but it is not. What does it mean to lead? Leadership is a specialization, just as mechanical engineering or information technology are specializations. To become a good leader, one must specialize in leadership. That means they have to learn various aspects of leadership and practice them endlessly. How they learn these aspects is immaterial. What matters most is that they practice them every day to increase the quality of their leadership and build up their capabilities as a leader. Despite what one may learn from books or others, good leadership is developed mostly through trial-and-error.

BE Today it is popular to say that leaders must practice their own version of standard work. Is this a good idea?

TO As time passes, there is an evolution in thinking as to what is necessary in order to make progress. All leaders practice some sort of standard work, though it may not be very good or not relevant to actual needs. In most cases, it is not written down as it is for an operator. Much of leaders' work is cyclic in nature, so standard work can certainly apply. Perhaps the time has come for leaders to write it down and follow it faithfully, as operators have long done. Of course, standards are the basis for improvement and must to be changed or updated as one thinks of new ideas or as circumstances change. Standard work will help leaders improve their practice of leadership for the cyclic as well as the non-cyclic work. It is obvious that standard work could be a big help to those who are charged with establishing TPS and to finally break free of 100-year old business methods that no longer serve needs. TPS is an unfamiliar way to do things, so standard work can help develop the new habit of mind and daily practice that is necessary to establish TPS as an overall management system for the company.

In What Ways Did This Conversation Improve Your Understanding of TPS?

-
-
-
-

How Will This Reduce Your Struggles?

-
-
-
-

Illusion of Knowledge

BE You speak about illusions of knowledge or illusions about knowing things. I would like to explore that a bit further. The reason why is that 100-year old business methods are still widely in use. How do we overcome that which is solidly entrenched and prevents needed progress?

TO What do we actually know? I believe we overestimate how much we know and we rely too much on what other people know. We rely on an architect to design our facility. We rely on a general contractor to build our facility. We rely on a machine tool maker to tell us how to cut metal. We rely on engineers to tell us how to design jigs and fixtures. We rely on accounting systems to tell us if we have made profits. We rely on computer systems to process information and tell us what has happened or make predictions. Most people do not understand these things. We assume the people who give these things to us understand them. Many things can make sense, but just because someone tells you how to do something or because it makes sense to you does not mean it is the right way to do things.

BE So one has to be skeptical?

TO Not just skeptical, but also has to test these things to assure that they actually meet one's needs. We must not assume that they meet our needs. I think it is safe to say that we over-estimate what we know. For example, I know how to make a wooden table. Or at least I think I do. I don't know for sure until I make a wooden table and discover the difficulties, one-by-one, that are sure to arise because there is a large gap between what I think or claim to know and what I actually know.

BE Why are we drawn to these illusions?

TO It is the result of being human. Overestimating our knowledge helps us ignore complexity. When we ignore complexity, we stop asking questions. But complexity must not be ignored. Complexity is expensive and error-prone, and it causes people to needlessly struggle. Complexity must be recognized so that people can work together to simplify things. Recall our earlier conversation, "Learn from Nature," where nature, through evolution, has devised simple solutions to complex problems. In business, the continuing use of 100-year old business methods show that evolution has not occurred with respect to the underlying thinking. Why not? Evolution is not the exclusive domain of nature. Obviously, the 100-year old business methods now use new technologies and are computerized rather than manual, but the underlying thinking that generates the methods remain. The underlying thinking is direct evidence of overestimating how much we know. We believe we have found the one and only answer, for all time. This is nonsense.

BE People are very satisfied when there is one answer or solution to a problem. They can then say "we're done" and relax or move on to something else. We have brains to find one answer, yet we don't use it to find other possible answers.

TO Being human does not mean we have no choice but to fall into various traps such as the illusion of knowledge. We must recognize that we can take action according to the various levels of details that one possesses. For example, a manager directs a course of action based on a limited understanding of a problem. Someone at a lower level in the company who possesses a detailed understanding of the problem might advise a different course of action. The point is, a general understanding is sufficient to take action, though it may be an incorrect action due to a lack of understanding of the details. If you make such mistakes in your personal life, then the effect is not great. But, if such mistakes are made in a company, then the effect can be great because it touches employees, suppliers, and others. This is why we must always question what we know. If we do not do that, then knowledge does not evolve, despite the fact that times have changed.

BE Previously, you spoke poorly of the sort of thinking that occurs in meetings or conference rooms.

TO Why do we think? It is to make a decision; to determine an action to take. The effectiveness of the decision will depend on the information one possesses. Consider these three options: First, one can think in the abstract and weigh different variables and make a decision. There are times when this level of thinking is appropriate. But, in most cases, it will lead to poor decisions. The second option is to think by making something physical with one's own hands, such as models or mock-ups, to improve decision-making. This is a deeper level of thinking. The third option is to think by actually making and testing new methods for doing work and evaluating which method has resulted in improvement. This option produces more information that is useful in decision-making than the previous two options. The first option is what most people do, and reflects the fact that they have overestimated how much they know; they see no need to try things before making a decision. The third option does not suffer from this overestimation of knowledge problem. It proceeds directly to trying out many ideas. The mindset in option 2 and 3 is "I don't know. Let's try it." while the mindset in option 1 is "I know."

BE In addition to overestimating one's knowledge, people overestimate their ability to predict an outcome.

TO Yes, people think they are very good at predicting outcomes, though their predictions are usually wrong. They favor making predictions over determining the root cause of abnormal conditions. It is impossible to predict the future, yet people put great effort into this, while they put little effort into basic root cause analysis, which is a useful source of information and learning that reduces one's overconfidence in what they know. I always tell people to work on what is difficult for them to do rather than what is easy for them to do. Predictions are easy but likely to be wrong. Trying things out is difficult because people are steadfast in their view that it is not necessary to try things out. They will make excuses that it takes too much time or costs too much money to try things out. People prefer to rely on their prediction capabilities, which stems from overestimating their knowledge. They must resist this and instead try things out.

BE The antidote to the illusion of knowledge is kaizen and trystorming, not prediction and brainstorming.

TO TPS would not have been established if we did what everyone else did. We had to develop methods that helped people overcome the human characteristic to overestimate one's knowledge. We had to create new types of physical experiences that put the facts in people's face: You don't know what you think you know. These experiences were learning-by-doing. When I say "try" or "trystorming," I mean "do."

BE So the way you overcame the natural tendency to overestimate one's knowledge was through kaizen. Yet, kaizen was the experience that generated new knowledge. And that knowledge could not be obtained in any other way.

TO "Kaizen" is often translated as "change for the better." Its actual meaning is "improve." Nevertheless, "change for the better," relates to one knowledge as well as to processes. Kaizen improves one's thinking and knowledge as well as processes or the method of doing things. The more kaizen one engages in, the more both thinking and doing improve. Fortunately, it is impossible for kaizen to result in the overestimation of one's knowledge. Kaizen thoroughly destroys that by revealing the infinite nature of improvement and the infinite nature of learning and discovery. Sometimes, it is useful to think of kaizen the opposite way: zenkai. Meaning, "better though change" or "better as a result of change," rather than "change for the better."

BE Kaizen takes away old knowledge and replaces it with new knowledge. And this new knowledge cannot be obtained any other way than by experiencing it.

TO The knowledge we hold most dear comes from our experiences. Illusions about raising children are shattered when one experiences it directly. The illusion that batch-and-queue processing is the best method is shattered when one directly creates and experiences flow. As I have said before, creating flow requires people to abandon preconceptions of knowledge. Because this is difficult to do, people usually need help.

BE Few people have directly experienced TPS. Therefore, most people's knowledge of TPS is based on what others have said.

TO It is possible for people to assume they know something because someone else knows something within their community. Knowing where to get information is not the same as knowing the information. But, again, I emphasize that knowing and know-how are the result of direct experiences. I place great importance on know-how.

BE In organizations, teamwork can substitute for knowing. Therefore, doesn't teamwork reinforce the illusion of knowledge?

TO It can if nothing is done about it. Kaizen teams often include members from other departments. And so one team member may have an abstract idea of what happens in that department. By bringing them together on kaizen teams, they have the opportunity to get to know each other and learn what the other does. Kaizen requires people to look closely at the work, so the abstract idea of what happens in that department dissolves and become concrete. Abstract ideas about the work performed are plentiful and must be transformed into fact. This helps develop teamwork and harmony between departments, and it improves information flow.

BE What about the illusion of understanding among top company leaders? Surely they suffer from illusions of understanding as well.

TO Yes. The further removed managers are from the genba, and the less contact they have with then genba over time, the more abstract their ideas are about what is actually happening on the genba. They make decisions based on abstract ideas about what is going on, not the facts. So I always emphasize that all managers must experience genba kaizen periodically to re-connect with the genba and understand what is actually going on. They must remove the abstract information in their brain and replace it with facts.

BE There is a reality television show called "Undercover Boss" that has been broadcast since 2010 in the United States. A top manager of the company poses as an entry-level employee and works on the front line for a week or so. Each episode proves how out of touch the leader is with what is actually going on at the genba. It is a painful show to watch. There have been 111 episodes so far. There are version of this show in many countries. The Japanese version, *Fukumen Research Boss Sennyū*, premiered in 2015.

TO That means there have been 111 CEOs who do not know the facts. That TV show could go on for another 1,000,000 episodes, or 70,000 years. This cannot continue; tolerance for poor leadership has grown immensely in recent decades. People think they can lead without knowing the facts. Or, they believe that facts they knew 20 years ago when they did such work are still relevant today. Or, they believe the information people given to them is the facts. These are big mistakes. They must go see for themselves. We cannot go on thinking we understand things that we do not actually understand. No improvement can occur when people are satisfied with existing situations.

BE In the digital age, what becomes of trystorming as a method for overcoming the illusion of knowledge?

TO Computer simulations reinforce the illusion of knowledge, so trystorming must continue. Trystorming must still be based on physical experiments or physical simulations. People will be tempted to perform computer simulations and stop there once they have the answer they want. But, computer simulations must be more deeply understood by physical simulations. And computer simulations must be verified by physical simulations.

BE People will see physical simulation as an unnecessary and time-consuming or expensive extra step.

TO Cook a simple meal in a computer simulation. Then try cooking that same meal in your kitchen. Take note of what you learned by actually cooking the meal in your kitchen.

In What Ways Did This Conversation Improve Your Understanding of TPS?

-

-

-

-

How Will This Reduce Your Struggles?

-

-

-

-

Developing People

BE You did what most supervisors no longer do, or, if they do it, most do not do it well. You developed people. But, you did that in an unusual way and developed capabilities in people that most other supervisors would never consider. Please tell me your thoughts on developing people and the method that you used.

TO In my duties as a manager, I felt I was not merely responsible for the output of our unit. I felt a deeper responsibility to the company, which means a responsibility to the people who are the source of corporate vitality. Therefore, I worked to develop the people who were under my supervision. But anyone can have this attitude. What is different is the combination of people and resources to do work that is required by individual customers. I felt that the focus of developing people should be the daily interplay between their intelligence and the resources they use to make things. Companies make big investments in equipment. The value of these investments are immediately reduced by 95 percent after installation because people do not know how to use these investments efficiently. The illusion of knowledge convinces people they know how to use these investments efficiently. But they do not. Thinking they know how to make things, people end up making things the most expensive way possible. In accounting, equipment depreciation allows the company to distribute the cost of the equipment over its useful life – where the useful life is determined by an accountant. As you may know, my views on the useful life of equipment are different – it has financial and productive value even it if the equipment has been fully depreciated. Regardless, I sought to increase the value of both the people and the equipment. While this increase in value is a fiction on the balance sheet, it is a reality on the genba. Value, in this case, is not merely money. My aim was to increase the combined value of people and equipment in human terms. If I allowed myself to be influenced by accountant's way of thinking, I would have never done this. But the genba is a different place than an accountant's spreadsheet. The genba is the truth, while a paper spreadsheet is merely a representation of the money aspect of various activities.

BE We have talked about the survival mentality that existed. How did this influence your approach to developing people?

TO Previously, we spoke about kaizen; Toyota-style IE. This was the basis for survival. It was our method for improving productivity and reducing costs. So we had to train people to understand the need for kaizen and how to practice kaizen. We were forced to do this by circumstances. There was no way that I could understand or correct all the problems we encountered. Our training had the objective of creating people who could autonomously run a process, identify abnormal conditions, and improve the process. But, we could not develop a few people to become experts. This would create bottlenecks for problem-solving. Instead, we tried to get as many people as possible trained in the method so that they would apply it to their circumstances and improve their process.

BE So what was your method for developing people?

TO First, let me focus on the beginning step of the method: Observation. People see things all day and don't actually know what is going on. They only think they know what is going on. So I would tell people to carefully observe a process for hours at a time. To convert their imagined understanding of the work to an actual detailed understanding of the work. Once they understood the current condition, I would challenge them by asking them: So now that you understand what is actually happening, tell me what should be happening? And so they would recite some things and I would listen intently. When they misunderstood or when their observation was incorrect or incomplete, I would scold them. If they were going in the right direction, I gave some vague signal to continue. I did not praise them because that would encourage them to stop. The capability I was developing in people was the ability to comprehend what is actually happening and challenging them to understand and state, in simple terms, what should be happening. This is fundamental. This is the crucial first step in my method for developing people. If this step does not take place, then subsequent development steps are useless. We use the term "normal condition" to describe what should be happening and "abnormal condition" for what should not be happening. The words "normal" and "abnormal" provide a frame of reference that does not exist when people say "problem" or "issue." Correction of a problem or issue may not result in a return to the normal condition because such a condition has not been clearly defined. Think about how bad the situation is in most companies: When you ask a worker what should   be happening, they tell you what is actually happening. The manager will tell you the same thing. There is no understanding or insight into what should be happening. Consequently, the work continues as usual, likely unchanged for years, thoroughly infused with all types of waste. This is how companies go broke. But before that happens, they harm workers though periodic pay cuts, layoffs and other drastic actions. This is no way to survive.

BE Observation leads to the development of an accurate understanding of reality; the actual working condition. From this, they can think of ideas for improvement. You want people to understand before they act.

TO Yes. But I want them to understand quickly; in hours or a few days, not weeks or months. Ideas for improvement are sure to be ineffective if the actual condition is not understood. I am sure you have seen many cases where corrections are made based on an abstract or assumed understanding of a problem. Or when people take action for the sake of taking action. That's no good. Improvement must be based on reality. That is why we came up with various means to improve the visibility of processes so that abnormalities are quickly revealed to anyone in the work area, as well as managers. No doubt you have seen many cases where corrections were made to surface-level problems. That too is no good. So we trained people to ask why five or more times to ascertain the root cause of the problem. Improvement based on an understanding of the root cause eliminates the abnormality, or reduces the frequency of its recurrence, which then allows people to observe, identify abnormalities, and think of more ideas for improvement. It has been said that we develop people to become idea factories for improvement. This is true, but with the understanding that ideas have clear targets and a clear purpose. It is not ideas for the sake of ideas.

BE I want to connect the thoughts about observation and the illusion of knowledge. Is it true to say that observation is the means by which you seek to destroy the illusion of knowledge?

TO That is true. People are adept at avoiding reality. So we take measures to make sure reality cannot be avoided. We develop people so that they are comfortable confronting reality. However, destroying the illusion of knowledge is useless if one does not take action to improve. So people development must expand to include practice in the kaizen method for making improvements. But, what is unique in our kaizen method is the use of human intelligence to devise simple, low cost improvements, and do so quickly. People are challenged to create find simple, low-cost improvements. Anyone can create complex, expensive solutions to problems. But that does not produce cost reduction or improve competitiveness. If I challenge a team to come up with a simple, low cost improvement, which they will do more easily than you can imagine, our countermeasure might cost $100 and take one day, while our competitors solution will cost $1,000,000 in new equipment and take one year. People do not realize the magnitude of the cost savings produced by our kaizen method. Because the company does not publicize these improvement miracles to outsiders, nobody knows about them. Eliminating an abnormality and returning to the normal condition cannot be expensive nor time-consuming. Spending money makes people feel good. My method trained people to not spend money and feel even better. They feel bad when they spend money because they did not meet their own personal challenge. Recall what I said earlier: The value of investments is reduced by 95 percent because people do not know how to use them efficiently, and that the focus of developing people is be the daily interplay between their intelligence and the resources available to make things.

BE People must be curious in order to improve. How do you develop curiosity?

TO We develop curiosity by asking people to ask why. Other companies are afraid of doing that because asking why causes many embarrassments to managers. People get blamed for asking why. So they suffer innumerable problems that go uncorrected for many years. They must stop that if they wish to survive. But there is more to it than just asking why. Our kaizen method leads people into new realm of understanding, a new way of thinking, that generates curiosity. One's own improvements, or improvements made by other teams, generates curiosity to learn and try new things. Trystorming and curiosity are connected. Both are needed. The result of our method for developing people is the development of new habits that they can apply autonomously as individual and in teams. Through practice, these habits become further ingrained and more effective over time. And they, in turn, train others. In this way, were able to make things quickly, at low cost, and with high quality.

BE One result of people development seems to be a remarkable ability for people, processes, and equipment to adapt to changing circumstances, including quickly re-arranging the work according to needs.

TO Manufacturing has many things thrown its way, from inside the company and from outside forces. We had to devise many methods to improve our flexibility, responsiveness, and adaptability at the individual level, department level, and so on. Things could not be fixed in place. We had to be able to move things around quickly. The thinking was always do-it-yourself, meaning you have the intelligence needed to make big improvements with none of   the usual resources. It also means to take personal responsibility for your work and improve it. This too pertains to survival. Many companies go bankrupt because they were unable to adapt to changing conditions. Seeing reality is more important than people realize.

BE Were top Toyota managers among the people you developed?

TO No, not directly. I had some influence through conversations and the results we achieved. My focus was on the work involved in making things that customers wanted. Making things was the target of actual need for survival. This approach to people development built the capabilities of future generations of leaders, which strengthened the competitiveness of the company. Those leaders instituted genba training for managers. Times are different now, so perhaps there is more than one target of actual need for survival. My approach to people development gave people a direction that they could understand and pursue. And their success, together, developed a spirit for improvement that prevails today. Yet, how many times do we see that money rolling into the company dulls the mindset and energy needed for survival. When that happens, managers lose interest in many important things such as developing people, operational efficiency, and so on.

BE There's no way this can be taught in school. Perhaps one can teach a familiarity or awareness, but never an understanding.

TO The classroom is the genba for the teacher, but it is not the genba for student. The student, if they work, have a genba to try things. But if they are young and in school full-time, then there is no genba. No genba means there is no place to try things and see what works. Manager's genba is their office and conference rooms. Here too there is no place to try things and see what works. So managers must move out of their offices and move into the genba. In sports, coaches are on the field, on the player's genba, not in an office. Sports team cannot be coached from an office, and neither can work teams. This is a simple fact.

BE What does one do with managers who want to stay in their offices?

TO Make them pay rent for their office and then they will move out instantly. Or take away their chair, desk, and everything else in the office. That will work too.

In What Ways Did This Conversation Improve Your Understanding of TPS?

-
-
-
-

How Will This Reduce Your Struggles?

-
-
-
-

Day Three
Conversation

Excuses

BE It is well known that you are intolerant of excuses. Many executives are intolerant of executes. But usually we do not understand exactly why executives are intolerant of excuses. Why are you intolerant of excuses?

TO Let us begin with a typical manager who is intolerant of excuses. They have work for 20 or 30 years in a chaotic environment that processes information using the batch-and-queue method. They do not know the true source or root of problems. And they do not use the problem-solving methods that they learned in earlier years. Their concern in relation to all these problems is how good or bad they look in their eyes of their boss and their peers. The interests of customers are not in their heart. Their personal interests, their own survival, occupy their heart and mind. So they are continuously grasping for any solution that they can claim as progress and that makes them look good. They need solutions, any solution, and they will not take excuses from anyone because they are worried about threats to themselves. Of course, not every manager is as I have described, but today it seems as if most are.

BE What you're describing is an intolerance for excuses that are rooted in a manager's desire for self-aggrandizement. I presume that your intolerance for excuses is not this.

TO I see excuses in relation to "Respect for Humanity." I will explain it in different ways. First, if people are making excuses, then it is a reflection that my efforts to develop them are not succeeding. Why? Second, when people make excuses, they express a lack of confidence in their own abilities. Human beings have great intelligence and are capable of things beyond what they can imagine. Third, excuses have an adverse effect on teamwork. Excuses become commonplace. Fourth, customers have needs that will never be satisfied with excuses. Fifth, excuses do not help the company survive. It pushes today's abnormal condition out to tomorrow or next year, and therefore gives control to others. You can no longer defend your own castle. And sixth, the company cannot be contributive to society if excuses are made.

BE So your intolerance for excuses is in relation to how it affects others, not how it affects you. And how it affects customers and consumes time.

TO Yes. In the time that people make excuses, they can try 10 or 100 ideas. Excuses eat time. My intolerance for excuses is also in relation to the idea of challenge. In business, there are many challenges to contend with. At work, you are receiving money from the company for your labor and your mind. To make excuses is to avoid using your mind. You are overpaid if only labor is given. You are cheating the company. And you are cheating yourself and others who depend on the company. In your personal life, you can make all the excuses you want for avoiding challenges. Nobody is paying you and the consequences are mostly yours alone to contend with.

BE Sometimes people make excuses because they don't know what to do. They are stuck. There is no method for moving forward.

TO This is why we develop people. To give them the training and practice to know what to do so that they do not come up with excuses and can instead move forward quickly. Only when you have thoroughly wracked you brain, squeezed it until nothing comes out, can you make an excuse. But, this can never actually happen. Excuses are avoidable through trystorming because it leads to many new ideas and possibilities. Brains are easily depleted by thinking alone. Trystorming quickly replenishes brains with dozens of new ideas. It inspires one's imagination.

BE Excuses, a lack of persistence, accepting things as they are, and not asking "why?" all seem to go together.

TO People give up too easily. So I had to push people hard so they could see that they had more intelligence and capability than they realized. When you contemplate developing people, excuses do not come to mind as a useful tool for the coach. I had to teach persistence. I had to teach improvement to break free of acceptance. I had to teach asking "why?" in order for people to eliminate abnormalities. These and other things are all connected. Perhaps this is why people struggle to establish TPS. We thought about this for many years and made constant corrections based on actual outcomes.

BE People make many excuses for not establishing TPS. They say it is too hard, or problems related to auto making or textile machines are not relevant to me, or we are a service business and don't manufacture anything, or 2017 is different and today's problems cannot be solved using 50- or 60-year old concepts and methods.

TO Age has nothing to do with usefulness. Stone is old and still very useful. These are excuses to do nothing different; to not improve. The world has indeed changed. However, many of the same fundamental problems remain with us because people continue to accepted things as they are. Today's solutions are built on top of yesterday's solutions, which were built on a base of faulty thinking, or thinking that did not evolve in step with changing times. I think also that what people see of TPS is merely the surface and they see the failures that companies have suffered. People avoid things that they think are bad. I warned long ago not to adopt only certain pieces of TPS. When this happens, disaster is certain, and word of such blunders quickly spread.

BE It is clear that people do not understand the deeper meaning or intent of TPS. How can this be corrected?

TO Isn't this book another such attempt? You learn the deeper meaning of something through practice, such as in music or sport or art. You have to put in the effort every day and focus on the elements of your work that need improvement. There is no mystery.

BE No mystery. But we again encounter excuses.

TO Excuses are an abnormal condition that plague organizations. Managers themselves must put effort into problem-solving to return to the normal condition. What are the root causes of managers' excuses and workers' excuses? Do you know? Managers must identify root causes and try many countermeasures for their excuses and workers' excuses. They will discover that management is responsible for the excuses they make and the excuses they receive. You want to be a manager! Therefore, you must take up such matters immediately and make concrete progress quickly. If one does not want to do this, then don't be a manager.

BE I imagine that some managers reading this book will think that digital transformation of their business means that much of what you have to say does not apply to them. They will make excuses. They will say there is no need for such-and-such.

TO Excuses are rooted in preconceptions. Rather than instantly conclude that such-and-such does not apply, think how it does apply given your unique circumstances. The likelihood is that it does apply, but you just have not yet figured out how. The need exists, but it is invisible for now. Dismissing things without consideration demonstrates managers' inability or lack of desire to think. This exposes the company and employees to unnecessary risks. So, have confidence in your intelligence and wrack your brain to make the invisible visible.

In What Ways Did This Conversation Improve Your Understanding of TPS?

-

-

-

-

How Will This Reduce Your Struggles?

-

-

-

-

Growing Sales

BE It seems managers are required to focus on growing sales and revenues. They say things like "grow or die" or "if you're not growing, you're going backwards." What are your thoughts on this growth imperative?

TO Who is asking for the company to grow sales? It is customers? No. Is it suppliers? No. Is it communities? No. Is it competitors? No. Is it investors? Yes. Investors are the group that is asking for sales and revenue growth. Most managers want this is well because they represent investors' interests, and compensation may be tied to growth targets. Why do investors want sales and revenue growth? Assuming growth is profitable, sales growth makes a company more valuable. It allows a company to take on new challenges, make new investments, and pay debts. It can improve competitiveness, create jobs, and increase incomes. A more valuable company is more difficult for others to take over because the price to buy it is high. Growth has many benefits. But it also has many pitfalls. And the rate of growth is of prime consideration.

BE Like many things in business, people focus on the upside and diminish or ignore possible downsides. What are some pitfalls associated with growth?

TO When management sets a course to achieve a certain sales growth target, this can become an all-consuming quest. Managers aim for quantity. This happened recently at Toyota. Management became obsessed with quantity and market share. They lost the essence of TPS for a while, which is to produce many models of vehicles in small quantities, tailored to individual needs. Any manager is happy when the cash rolls in, but this success causes blindness. Success hides problems, the long-term becomes sacrificed for short-term gains in sales growth, they seek economies of scale, they diversify into lines of business that they know nothing about, they acquire other businesses under false assumptions such as "synergies," and, importantly, managers play numbers games to strengthen the appearance of growth.

BE Any other pitfalls?

TO Of course. Sales growth tempts managers to ignore the buyers' market they face and try to gain advantage for themselves by creating a sellers' market. They will also try to take advantage of customers in various ways, such as giving them fewer choices. They will use expensive marketing and advertising to get customers to buy things they do not need. The company always takes on more debt. And complacency sets in. The drive to grow sales can last many years, which trains people to do the things required to grow sales. When sales slow or the economy goes into recession, people do not know how to adjust. They developed skills for high growth, not for low growth or decline. They don't know what to do. So the company suffers greatly when growth inevitably stalls.

BE So growth is not all upside. Why don't managers recognize the downsides? In one reads *The Wall Street Journal* every day, you'll easily come across many stories of serious problems that have arisen in pursuit of sales growth.

TO It seems most managers think they are some kind of hero and can succeed at anything merely because they are a manager. As one goes higher in the company, they are awarded certain privileges that makes them haughty. They lose touch with customers and they lose touch with the employees and the work that satisfies customers. Soon, they think the impossible can be achieved overnight and with no ill consequences. This is a detachment from reality that sooner or later will cause harm.

BE What, then, is your overall view of sales and revenue growth?

TO To be sure, of sales and revenue growth are important markers of success. That is undeniable. The question is: What is rate of growth? Beginning with the days of corporate raiders, it has been fashionable for managers to pursue double-digit growth. Managers seek 10 or 20 percent annual growth or higher, maybe 50 or 75 percent. The highest growth rates are typically the result of serial acquisitions. This is an expensive and disruptive way to grow. My view is that stable long-term growth should be the objective. This means annual growth rates of two to four percent. Higher growth rates cause instabilities that are distracting and difficult for managers to contend with. Financial problems are sure to arise.

BE What form should the growth take?

TO Sales growth must be the result of satisfying individual customer's needs better than the competition. So it should come from within; so-called organic growth. Use the cash generated from sales to make investments that lead to additional growth. This form of investment develops internal capabilities that strengthen competitiveness. Human resources are developed in tandem with growth. Problems arise when growth increases at a faster rate than human resources can be developed. The mismatch reflects the fact that learning takes time, while high growth can be achieved quickly. Just because high growth can be achieved quickly does not mean one should pursue it. Humans cannot catch-up easily to the demands of high growth. Stable long-term growth enables managers and workers to respond more effectively to changes in market conditions. Consider the concept of Just-in-Time applied to growth, where the need is match or synchronized to the capability. Do you know what the word "Just" means in Just-in-Time? Most people don't know. They think it clarifies what "In-Time" means. That is incorrect. "Just" refers to the material consumed in production. It means what is needed in the amount needed. Produce just what is needed in the amount needed; no more. "In-time" means when needed. If the meaning of "Just" is not understood, then myriad types of waste are produced, not eliminated.

BE Thank you for that clarification. I think many people misunderstand what Just-in-Time means, which adds to their struggles. Managers' interest in high growth is connected to the idea that management has a responsibility to maximize returns to investors. What do think of that business objective?

TO Who is asking for such a stupid thing? Investors. They are a special interest group. Managers who blindly follow the needs of a special interest group are bound to get the company into trouble. Investor's preconceived notions must not automatically transfer to management. Instead managers must think! Maximizing returns to shareholders discourages management from making investments for current and future times. It discourages them from allocating resources properly, to assure survival. Any fool should be able to figure out that in business, things cannot actually be maximized. To maximize returns to investors means you must eliminate all debt. But at any point in time, the company owes money to employees, suppliers, government, and so on. Human and economic needs must be balanced. Imbalances create waste. Sales growth, while much desired, must be carefully managed. If mismanaged, unfavorable knock-on effects become widespread both within the company and outside the company.

BE In addition to improving productivity, managers expect that digitization of business processes will drive sales growth. What are your thoughts on this?

TO By itself, digitizing business processes will have very limited impact on sales growth. But, digital processes that satisfy individual customers' needs – giving customers exactly what they want, in the amount wanted, when they want it – has great potential to grow sales. Every company will seek to do this. The question then becomes: How does one do this better than one's competitors? This will require human intelligence and ingenuity, and the ability to rapidly respond to changing customer tastes and needs. Conventional management practice has not prepared managers for this new challenge.

In What Ways Did This Conversation Improve Your Understanding of TPS?

-

-

-

-

How Will This Reduce Your Struggles?

-

-

-

-

Pursuit of Scale

BE Economies of scale is a preconceived notion that is deeply embedded in the minds of managers. Your work tells us this way of thinking and making things is incorrect. What are your thoughts on economies of scale?

TO I have said that excess inventory is the greatest waste of all. Any concept or practice for making things that produces excess inventory is no good. Because the batch-and-queue method leads to high costs at low production volumes, managers order the production of larger quantities. But if a company serves buyers' markets, then the excess will go unsold, resulting in higher costs and lower profits. They must find ways to liquidate the excess, all of which increase costs and generate no profit or produce losses. Why would you do such a stupid thing? Manages are attracted to economies of scale because it allows them to take it easy and live under the illusion that they serve sellers' markets. It is worse than an illusion. It is a perpetual delusion to think that all one has to do to reduce unit costs – to drive down the fixed cost portion of unit costs – is to produce more. It is a simple cost-volume relationship that is easy to apply. There is no skill in that. I train people to understand that it is not necessary to make more than what is needed, in the amount needed, when it is needed. Our efforts developed practical methods for doing that.

BE Economies of scale relies on simple calculations.

TO Simple calculations confirm the validity of economies of scale. But many times I have warned against simple calculations because the numbers can deceive. Managers must be alert to simple calculations that confirm their bias for taking it easy and desire to boast about the output and the scale of their operations. Nobody cares about that except the manager. Instead of sticking with a process and merely producing more as the method for reducing costs, we abandoned that method and sought to reduce both unit and total costs by using better methods. It is remarkable that even today, managers do not understand this concept, which is based on realism: Method A yields unit cost A. Method B yields unit cost B. Method C yields unit cost C. Method Z yields unit cost Z. Some methods reduce both unit and total costs. Sticking to a method that has the appearance of reducing unit costs but increases total costs is foolish.

BE Economies of scale is widely understood to be the savings of resources that comes from large scale production. Resources include money, material, equipment, space, energy, labor, time, and so on.

TO Such assumptions must be tested rather than blindly accepted. It is obvious that costs depend on many variables. How can it depend on only one variable, volume? It is irresponsible to run a business based on 7th grade math.

BE The famous economies of scale curve is in every economics textbook and most business school textbooks on the subject of operations.

TO Books can be dangerous. The economies of scale curve is a graphical description of the amortization of unit costs over volume using the batch-and-queue production method. If one does not use the batch-and-queue method, then the economies of scale curve is irrelevant. The curve has no meaning. Therefore, the concept and the curve must be abandoned. Managers who retain this idea will be unable to achieve smooth flow. Flow is the lowest total cost way of making things. Accounting systems used today were developed in times of sellers' markets and batch-and-queue processing. So the numbers will always deceive and tell managers the unit cost is higher for flow production. But management is not responsible solely for unit cost. They are responsible for total costs as well. Companies go broke when total costs exceed revenues, not when unit costs exceed revenues. Managers will complain about high unit costs and blame operations as if it is the only source of cost in the company. That is nonsense. All departments are a source of cost for the company. Management's focus must be on total costs. If that is their focus, then they will pursue flow relentlessly. TPS, applied as an overall management system, enables all departments to contribute to profit through cost reduction and productivity improvement.

BE Can you give an example of where numbers deceive?

TO Ocean transport, shipping, is plagued with economies of scale thinking. Container ships get ever-larger in shipping companies efforts to reduce unit costs for their customers. But as ships grown in size, docks must be built, channels dredged and deepened, larger cranes are needed, bigger tug boats, more terminal land for storing full and empty container, more trucks and trailers and rail cars to move containers, expanded road and rail infrastructure, more capital equipment, more financing and fees, and so on. The simple economics of container shipping leads to complex and costly problems that customers pay for through their contracts with shipping companies. But this is not always true. Ocean freight has been a commodity business, so prices go up or down based on demand, not actual costs. When demand is up, prices and capacity go up. When demand is down, prices and capacity go down. So has unit cost actually been reduced? The numbers many say "yes," but the numbers deceive. People forget about time delays associated with moving containers from here to there, and losses when containers fall off the ship or when the ship sinks. Shipping companies are consolidating these days to reduce competition and gain pricing power. So all the effort put into to reduce unit costs over many years has had no beneficial result for customers who use container ships. They should consider local or regional sourcing instead.

BE The subtitle to the English version of TPS is "Beyond Large-Scale Production." What does it that mean?

TO Managers' thinking is tied to economies of scale. But my work has shown that managers should not pursue scale; that they must abandon management based on scale. The success of TPS justifies our decision abandon management based on scale. Other managers can use this same justification and realize myriad benefits as we have.

BE That begs the question, what are the downsides of TPS?

TO With TPS, we try to create a system that mimics nature because, though difficult to establish, it is simpler and more intuitive. Humans are a product of nature. We automatically responding to abnormal conditions such as thirst, hunger, an itch, a grain of sand in our eye, and so on. TPS is human-like in this way. So asking what are the disadvantages of TPS is similar to asking what are the disadvantages of being human. Like anything, there may be some disadvantages. But are the disadvantages correctable or are they structural? TPS evolved in a way that makes disadvantages, abnormalities, easily recognizable and correctable. Being flexible and adaptable, I cannot think of any structural disadvantages in TPS itself. Perhaps one example that it takes curiosity, energy, imagination, and enthusiasm for TPS to evolve once it is established. Many people misunderstand TPS and practice it poorly, so they suffer many disadvantages. Therefore, a disadvantage is that TPS is difficult to understand and do. I think this is the biggest problem, because all other problems come from that. For example, if TPS is misunderstood, then workers are driven harder, which is an abnormality. Instead, workers' job must be made easier. If economies of scale mindset or other preconception associated with common management practice exists when trying to establish TPS, then the disadvantages will multiply. I urge managers to begin TPS by eliminating preconceived notions. Any fixed notions, such as economies of scale, constitute structural disadvantages to improvement and progress.

BE Economies of scale is another case where managers see all upside and no downside.

TO Previously, I have criticized thinking, but the things we have been talking about show the need for thinking in relation to reality. The simple economics of economies of scale is not so simple. Why should unit costs go down when volume goes up? It this always the case? No. Why is this so? Economies of scale requires expensive capital equipment and annual service contracts. It encourages buying more material than is actually needed in order to get a lower price. There will be more inventory between processing steps and many expenses associated with managing inventories. There will be warehouses for raw materials and for finished goods. Costly sales incentives will be required in order to sell what has been overproduced. Items that don't sell must be liquidated for a fraction of production costs, while obsolete items will be recycled or scrapped. Has scale really lowered unit costs? Managers have trouble realizing that scale is no good if you cannot sell what you have produced for a profit. They overproduce because it makes their budget numbers look better and makes production look more efficient, not because sales have increased.

BE How does TPS overcome this?

TO Fundamentally, TPS is a buyers' market, demand-driven production system. Our goal is to make only what we can sell; meaning, sell one, make one, using flow production methods. Economies of scale reflects the thinking associated with batch-and-queue production. Batch-and-queue is a sellers' market, supply-driven production system. Its goal is to make as much as possible. That is sensible when 100 percent of the quality produced can be sold. But such marketplaces do not exist any longer, except in rare cases. When financial difficulties arise, managers commonly say: "Every element of cost must be scrutinized." I never hear managers say: "Every process needs to be quickly improved." Costs are subordinate to processes. This is another thing that managers find difficult to understand.

BE Economists do not help matters. They continue to believe in the effectiveness of the batch-and-queue production method and seem to know nothing about flow.

TO This is true. Many business people listen to economists. It is remarkable for them to think that cost is independent of the production method used. This is the result of calculating numbers in an office instead of going to the genba to see one-piece flow with one's own eyes.

BE What would you say to economists? And to managers?

TO I would say simply this: There is more for you to learn. The shape of the economies of scale curve is the result of long machine set-up times, long queue times, long transportation times, and large cycle time mismatches between operations and between processes. These are abnormal conditions, none of which are fixed. Each element of time can be reduced and synchronized. The economies of scale curve is rendered obsolete when set-up time, queue time, and transportation time have been reduced from days or weeks to minutes or hours, and when cycle time mismatches have been eliminated. Flow turns the curve into a nearly flat horizontal line, which allows low volumes to be produced at low cost. People imagine the economies of scale curve as a single curve. That is incorrect. There are actually a family of curves who shape depends upon the production method used. The L-shaped curve contains a deep knee for batch-and-queue production method and a flat horizontal line for flow. In between is other production methods that are a mix of the two that yield different shapes, between the L-shaped curve and the flat horizontal line. I would tell economists and managers that they need to understand and promote flow because that method is lowest cost, and it enables one to produce small numbers of items in many varieties to satisfy the requirements of individual customers. It brings the company in closer touch to the marketplace. And it brings the company in closer harmony with nature and its available resources. This will become a clear need in the near future.

BE We talked about scale in the context of output and large capital equipment used to produce physical items. What about economies of scale in relation to computing?

TO Our approach is to use the smallest and least expensive machine necessary to do what is required. If customer demand increases, we improve productivity first, followed by adding more of these types of small, low cost machines to the line. Computing follows a similar logic in terms of adding machines. If customer demand generates a need for increased computing capability, machines should be added in the smallest increments necessary to do what is required. Because the rate of change is so great in computing, buying more computing capability than necessary increases costs and risks loss of investment due to rapid obsolescence. Don't buy extra computing power just to get a lower unit price. Always keep this in mind: How do you make things that customers desire at a low cost? Over-buying or renting more computing power than is needed increases costs.

In What Ways Did This Conversation Improve Your Understanding of TPS?

-

-

-

-

How Will This Reduce Your Struggles?

-

-

-

-

Flow

BE The vast majority of production systems are initially set-up as batch-and-queue and stay that way for many years. The concept of flow in manufacturing, or in any productive activity, is an extremely simple concept. Yet it is rare to find flow. This suggests that it is difficult to create a system where material and information flows, which, in turn, accounts for the persistence of batch-and-queue production.

TO What is flow? Flow is the normal condition. Anything that impedes flow is an abnormality. What is the normal condition? It is when the required material and the required information flow smoothly, continuously, uninterrupted, from one step in the process to the next. For this to occur, a basic condition must be satisfied: The cycle times for each operation must be less than the takt time, or rate of customer demand, and cycle time must be balanced to reduce operator waiting time. There are two understandings of flow: 1) Flow of a sequence of operations within a process and 2) Flow between processes. In TPS, flow must exist within a sequence of operations and between processes. Many companies do kaizen and achieve flow within a process. That is not good enough. They must also establish flow between processes. They must connect upstream processes to downstream processes. That is much more difficult to do. It requires relentless trial-and-error efforts. Think of it as streams that flow into a river that flows to an estuary that flows to the ocean.

BE People see flow in final assembly, but upstream processes are batch-and-queue. Or, flow may exist in upstream processes but final assembly is batch-and-queue. They are hybrids of batch-and-queue and flow.

TO These types of hybrid production are not what I mean by flow. They lack the necessary synchronization between operations and processes. Interrupted flow is not flow. Continuous flow is flow. That is what one must strive to achieve. Sometimes continuous flow is not possible due to various constraints. So we developed methods to contend with interruptions and maintain smooth flows. While hybrid production can be lower cost than batch-and-queue, it is higher cost than flow. Even though hybrid production is better than batch-and-queue production, one must not stop there because it limits the ability to satisfy customers and response to changing conditions will remain sluggish.

BE In the pursuit of flow, it is common to see many companies continue using conventional management methods.

TO Somehow, it is not obvious to managers that management methods must change to support the new production flow methods The two must change together. The persistence of management for batch-and-queue when efforts are made to establish flow is an effect that has many causes.

BE Care to identify a few causes?

TO Managers like to establish controls to give them a sense of command or authority over people and processes and to justify their position as someone charged with responsibility to say "yes" or "no." Batch-and-queue production, being chaotic and expensive, requires control by managers to decide what to make, how much to make, and when to make it, and to be the ones who say "yes" or "no." In TPS, we developed methods for customers to be the ones who say "yes" or "no." They tell us what to make, how much to make, and when to make it. And operators are also given the ability to "yes" or "no" in terms of product quality – stop the line – and process improvement – trystorming. Because of this, we have many fewer managers than other companies. Managers are very expensive employees. So we have reduced this expense by creating a production system that requires less management. This is something that people seem to be unaware of. It allows us to deploy management resources differently than in other companies. We can staff management positions that enable us to study and do things to develop our competitive capabilities that others companies cannot.

BE People often say that what employees do at work they would never do at home. In other words, at home they have autonomy and do things that make sense, but at work they are controlled through hierarchies and do things that do not make sense, such as batch-and-queue processing.

TO Hierarches automatically make people afraid to think or do things. To create flow, you have to be able to think and do things; you have to be able to experiment and try things. Like every other company, we had hierarchy but were able to develop people to think and to rapidly try out their ideas.

BE Even though people were afraid of you.

TO Yes. Being afraid of a superior out of respect is different than being afraid of a superior out of disrespect. Being afraid of a superior whose guidance is sound is different than being afraid of a superior whose guidance is inconsistent or incoherent. The first causes thinking and action while the second causes stoppages and stagnation.

BE Let's return to what people do at work compared to what they do at home in relation to flow or lack of flow.

TO At home, you don't buy 50 times more food than you need just to obtain lower prices. And you have no place to put all that food. When you make dinner consisting of protein, starch, and vegetable, you don't make the 50 times the amount of protein you need and let it sit for a few days or weeks. You don't make 50 times the amount of starch you need and let it sit for a few days or weeks. You don't make the 50 times the amount of vegetable you need and let it sit for a few days or weeks. Instead, you make what is needed in the amount needed at the time it is needed. In manufacturing, people make things and then let them sit around days or weeks or months. Why not instead immediately move a completed item to the next step? When you prepare a meal, the things you need are in close proximity. You put plates in the kitchen, not in the bedroom. You don't put your pots and pans in the house next door. In manufacturing, operators have to search for needed items and tools, and fixtures are stored someplace far from where they are actually used. Why does the company pay skilled people to walk around and find things, thereby lowering productivity, increasing costs, and reducing profits? Home-life is not a perfect analogy for how to do things in the workplace, but it offers some important clues.

BE Often, a job must be expedited to meet a customer's need that suddenly arose. A familiar example is the purchase order process. When someone really needs a purchase order, they walk it through the process and complete it in an hour instead of days or weeks.

TO To this I say, if you can complete the work in an hour on a special occasion, why can't you do it that way every day? What the expediting did was to eliminate waste in the process. Expediting a job gives an indication of the maximum amount of time a job actually takes. But never be satisfied with just that. With additional observation and experimentation, more waste can be eliminated. In this way, competitiveness is improved.

BE Managers make things difficult for operations when workloads are shaped like a saw-tooth. Work is slack for the first two weeks of the month, and then people are busy for the last two weeks of the month. This disrupts work and causes innumerable other problems. Managers think the company can succeed under such circumstances. What do you say about that?

TO People who become managers quickly lose touch with what is actually going on. As a result, they do not recognize the trouble that such circumstances cause to workers. Nor do they see the trouble it causes to suppliers and customers and investors. Management is blind to abnormal conditions when they have no sense of what the normal condition should be. They ignore workers' struggles as if workers are required to struggle. This old mindset cannot carry forward into the future. In TPS, production leveling is basic way of thinking. It is foundational to the successful functioning of TPS. Do you starve yourself for two weeks and then eat food for two weeks? No! A management that cannot change its thinking will doom the company. It is easy to generate the appearance of success to outsiders, but such companies will limp along for many years because there is no vitality among the workers inside the company. Stupidity can be deeply entrenched. Abandoning stupidity reveals to everyone that you have been stupid for many years. Voluntarily exposing one's stupidity to others is a better alternative than remaining stupid.

BE It seems workers are never eager to convert their work to flow. If they saw benefits, they might make efforts to create flow. Why don't they see flow as a logical and sensible way to do work? In other words, why is there no demand for flow among workers. We understand why managers reject flow. But why do workers?

TO When people join a company, management assigns them a task. The newly hired personnel, seeking to conform and maintain employment, do the work as instructed by management. And they assume that someone else studied the work and determined the way they have been shown to do the work is the best way. So they do as they are told. We do this as well. But the difference is that we train people to understand that the work they do can be improved forever, and that they and their team must aggressively pursue improvement every day. They are trained in the methods of improvement and given the authority to eliminate waste and improve flow without having to contend with company bureaucracy. I believe workers have an innate desire to make their job easier and perform it with fewer errors. It is management's responsibility to cultivate worker's desire for improvement, not to shut it down.

BE It is common today that companies establish bureaucracies to oversee improvement efforts. Individuals and teams spend a great deal of time analyzing work and then present their findings to management in order to get permission to move forward. Many companies apply ratings to work areas to indicate the level of improvement achieved such as Bronze, Silver, and Gold. This has been the evolution of improvement practice in many large companies.

TO This is all wrong. It is de-evolution, not evolution. In English, kaizen is interpreted as "continuous improvement." Improvement will cease when Gold level is reached. People must be free to quickly analyze the work and make small improvements every day without seeking permission. Requiring permission terminates the spirit needed for improvement and will not result in human development and capability-building. Companies face competition, so improvement must occur lightning-quick. Bureaucracy overseeing improvement activities has no purpose but to slow down improvement, increase costs, and diminish competitiveness. Management review may be needed in special cases such as when the breadth or scale of the improvement idea is significant, it spans multiple departments, and it requires coordinated efforts to make the required product and process changes. Even when such review is needed, it must be done quickly. Management should want to generate flow within and between processes as soon as possible. Their bureaucratic interference will only slow things down.

BE Investors, generally, do not demand flow either. There are a few who understand TPS, but they are not very influential among their peers. I think it is strange, given the narrow interests of investors which usually centers around costs, profits, growth, and market share, that they favor batch-and-queue and do not recognize flow. The fact is, flow is a better way to fulfill the interests of investors.

TO It is. I cannot speak to the mindset of investors, other than to say it must somehow reflect the thinking that comes from economists and other who have influence on money matters. I have long battled accountants and others who firmly believe in the numbers even though the genba contradicts the numbers. Flow goes against conventional thinking and investors, like most others who understand only numbers, are locked into preconceptions and see no benefit to altering their views. Despite this, efforts must be made to teach investors about flow.

BE Perhaps if managers, workers, and investors thought about what problems they were trying to solve, they would discover much common ground and recognize flow as a solution.

TO The problem that we were trying to solve is, as I have said previously, to produce different items in small quantities tailored to individual needs. Many companies, perhaps most, have this same problem. Therefore, TPS can be practiced by most companies. We found that flow solves numerous problems that are of interest to various people: the employees, the suppliers, the customers, the investors, and the community in which the business operates. Flow is a countermeasure to common problems found in most business that face fierce competition, such as efficiency, cost, time, quantity, quality, teamwork, and more. What business serving competitive buyers' markets does not have cost reduction as a goal?

BE So TPS is an omnibus solution to common business problems. I think that this is not widely recognized, nor is there much demand for this type of solution from company leaders. They seem to prefer point solutions that satisfy a single need, and do not care if the solutions to different problems are disconnected from one another or if they contradict each other.

TO It is true that there are many competing methods for solving common business problems. I would have thought time might have had a hand in sorting out the methods that strengthen competitiveness versus those methods that weaken competitiveness.

BE I don't think CEOs see any method as weakening competitiveness. I believe they think all methods strengthen competitiveness. To them, it's just a question of which method to use when.

TO They must abandon their preconceptions, as that clearly cannot be true. I have said many times before that TPS came from need. TPS will not be established if there is no need. Management will use other methods based on need. The fact that TPS is an effective countermeasure for many common business problems is meaningless if management does not recognize the need for TPS.

BE Can you please summarize why you say TPS will work for any type of business?

TO The fundamental activity performed by any business, large or small, is material and information processing. Yet, if one views material as a form of information, then it becomes clear that information processing is the core of business activity. This means that any distinction between manufacturing and service disappears, making TPS universal in its application. TPS is an information processing system.

BE The manufacturing-service distinction has been a significant barrier for adopting TPS in service businesses.

TO What I have described earlier is how TPS takes a scientific approach to management – asking questions, clear problem statements, experimenting, fact-based decisions, and so on. This approach is universal in its application. There is no restriction whatsoever. The scientific method has innumerable merits over the gut instinct method or the political method commonly used by managers. The basis for judgment and decision-making is more sound for TPS than for conventional management, whether it is leader or a worker on the shop floor or in the office. With TPS, everyone feels a responsibility for cost reduction, not just managers. Everyone feels a responsibility for flexibility, adaptability, and responsiveness, not just managers. Everyone feels a responsibility for survival, not just managers. TPS strengthens competitiveness and helps assure survival in bad times. Why? Because TPS is the least resource-intensive way to process information. It teaches, for example, methods for information processing that require the least investment. While the competition throws away large sums of money on equipment that is not needed or which over-processes and overproduces, TPS allows you to do the same work better at lower cost and with higher quality.

BE Company leaders are rapidly investing in digitizing business processes because it results in information flow without the time or expense needed to improve physical processes. They can eliminate physical processes.

TO Time and expense are needed to digitize processes, and I am certain that many physical processes will be digitized unnecessarily. Digitizing is a process improvement only to the extent that the software people understand the process. It is possible for software specialists to digitize processes and impair information flow. Improvement is not the automatic outcome. People who have experience in improving physical processes via kaizen must learn software basics and work with software specialists to assure that the desired outcomes are achieved. And software specialists must participate in genba kaizen to understand physical processes and to develop the mindset of improvement that results in low costs, and apply that knowledge when they create software.

In What Ways Did This Conversation Improve Your Understanding of TPS?

-

-

-

-

How Will This Reduce Your Struggles?

-

-

-

-

Day Four
Conversation

Training and Practice

BE You have said that training and practice are essential elements for the establishment and evolution of TPS. Why is this so?

TO Take the example of professional sports. One cannot succeed without extensive training and practice. To compete requires a strong spirit to take on challenges and a commitment to endure the required training. With the proper mindset and training, the skills that have been practiced become instinct. Winning cannot be achieved in the absence of these characteristics. For a company to succeed, the people must be motivated to face the competition and trained in methods needed to succeed. Just as an athlete makes a commitment to training the mind and body, managers must make a commitment to train the mind and body of all employees. Training must be consistent and never-ending.

BE In recent years, companies have reduced their investment in training led by people. Or they have sought less expensive training methods such as computerized training and now virtual reality.

TO Reducing training to save money reflects decisions that are made by looking at numbers without understanding the need or ignoring the need. Oftentimes, management cuts costs in the short-term and sacrifices the long-term. Training is an easy budget item to cut. It is inevitable that computer training and the emergence of methods such as virtual reality will become part of training as their cost declines and their effectiveness improves. However, computer-based training must not totally replace training in the physical world – on the genba. For now, there are differences, and so both are necessary. As I said earlier, TPS is established when there is a need for TPS. Training, whether it is virtual and real, must support that need, and practice must be based on the training.

BE Training for TPS is a type of specialization or specialized training that differs greatly from general management training. An analogy might be that TPS is the type of training one undergoes to run a marathon, while conventional management is the type of training one undergoes to run in sprint races.

TO That is a reasonable analogy. The marathoner runs at a speed of about 20 kilometers per hour, while the sprinter runs at about double that speed. If the two were to race against one another over some distance, the sprinter would have to rest after every sprint while the marathoner would continue along. In a short time, time, the marathoner would be far ahead and eventually win. TPS and the training for TPS reflects the marathon, while conventional management reflects the sprint. In TPS, we work to achieve a smooth continuous flow, while conventional management favors batch-and-queue, meaning sprinting: start-stop-start-stop-start-stop. Therefore, TPS training for management and workers is to help them become marathoners, not sprinters. TPS becomes fully established when all employees become marathoners. This is a source of competitive strength, because, in this analogy, the race in business is long, not short. That is why we value our employees. They have received specialized training that cannot be obtained anywhere else.

BE Yet, these days, many company leaders not want to invest in people. Employees are seen as a disposable resource. Training is seen as a poor investment because people will quickly leave the company if they receive a better offer. There is little in the way of loyalty, company to employee or employee to company.

TO Because our employees have received specialized training, we do not lay them off as sales fluctuate. The mindset and skills cannot be found in the labor market. Unfortunately, companies whose employees receive little training can be fired and easily replaced by others when business picks up. We cannot do that.

BE I think most managers would prefer to avoid specialized training and have the flexibility to fire and hire workers as business volumes fluctuate. I imagine that will change and computer-based training costs drops and as it demonstrates it effectiveness more quickly.

TO Of course. This is the mindset of a sprinter who does not realize or does not care that they are actually running a marathon, not a sprint. They do not understand how to build competitive capabilities. These same managers will lay people off due to productivity improvement, thereby eroding their competitiveness and derailing their efforts to establish TPS. These are self-inflicted wounds. In our way of thinking, management betrays workers if they lay people off due to productivity improvement. This must not happen. The consequences are too severe.

BE Don't these problems reflect the fact that that conventional management has a strong preference for quick and easy answers, as opposed to the hard work of training and practice?

TO This is merely part of being human. But another part of being human is to resist temptations for easy answers and put in the effort necessary to develop the mindset and skills that enable continuing success. This is especially important for managers because they lead people. That is a big responsibility.

BE Sadly, it is my experience that most managers don't see it as a big responsibility. They have different views.

TO The responsibility is similar to being a parent. Of course, there are many bad parents, but people must not be promoted into management positions if they are unable to recognize and properly attend to their responsibilities.

BE Isn't taking responsibility part of the TPS training?

TO Yes. We hold individual responsibility in high regard, as well as our collective responsibility to society. This, apparently, is difficult for others to do. Why? Perhaps this helps people further understand how TPS differs from conventional management: Problems are the raw material of management decision-making. We have found that improving processes means fewer errors or abnormalities are generated which, in turn, means fewer decisions need to be made by managers. Yet, more problems do not necessarily mean managers make more decisions. In fact, more problems mean decisions will not be made, decisions will be delayed, or that bad decisions will be made. In all three cases, decision-making is plagued by defects. Too many decisions lead to a paralysis or inability to make good decisions. This affects one's ability to fulfill responsibilities at any level, from individual to team to department to company to society. TPS, as an information system, is a method for reducing the volume of management decisions and improving the quality of decisions, which then enables management to focus on practicing other skills such as observation, developing people, and so on. This strengthens the mind for decision-making and increases the speed and effectiveness of decision-making. By focusing on the basics, we build a strong foundation.

BE The chaotic batch-and-queue environment generates lots of problems requiring many decisions. The training that companies use to help improve decision-making under such conditions seems ineffective.

TO Likely that is so. Computer-based training and virtual reality will not change that outcome. We chose a path that was more difficult to master initially, but which has yielded much better results. Think of training in martial arts or a musician's training. Learning is difficult at first but rewarding in the long run. TPS is like that.

BE And music, of course, must flow. People don't learn to play music so that they can play something that does not flow.

TO Anyone can play batch-and-queue music. It is not enjoyable to listen to and customers will not buy it. It does not make sense to train people for things that do not result in pleasing customers. If you visit Toyota, you will see various physical devices for training and practice to develop certain skills. You are unlikely to see these in any other company. This gives an indication of the importance that we place on training and how it must be related to needs. Employees design and make these unique training tools, which is yet another example of their imagination, ingenuity, and creativity.

BE I believe virtual reality will fundamentally change the nature of training for TPS. I understand that practice on the genba must obviously continue because only improvements made in the real world contribute to cost reduction and productivity improvement. But TPS concepts, methods, and ways of thinking that have been difficult to describe in books, difficult teach in classrooms, or that people have otherwise struggled to understand and implement might be easily corrected by virtual reality training – an immersive experiential method of training similar to genba kaizen. Maybe then TPS becomes more widely accepted as the management system to replace conventional management. If not virtual reality, then neurotechnology will surely do it.

TO If that is the case, then there is no need to write more books about TPS. The era of using books to teach people TPS has come to an end. I know from experience that it is easier to change or update software than printed books. Therefore, training people in TPS using virtual reality seems to be an improvement. What is neurotechnology?

In What Ways Did This Conversation Improve Your Understanding of TPS?

-

-

-

-

How Will This Reduce Your Struggles?

-

-

-

-

Stagnation vs. Evolution

BE It is remarkable how processes in conventional businesses remain fixed for many years or even decades. Little or no change occurs despite changing people, changing times, and changes in the marketplace.

TO Companies that do not change with the times suffer the consequences. Stagnant conditions reveal a management that insists on controlling things and assuring a minimum of disturbances. Management has a responsibility to promote daily evolution in response to the ever-changing competition that it faces. This is what a coach does for an athlete. This is what managers must do for one another and for workers.

BE The leaders of companies that are stagnant would resist that characterization and point to many examples of their evolution.

TO Managers often cite purchases of expensive new equipment or software as evidence of evolution, or changes in processes that increase complexity and waste. One must carefully scrutinize such claims. They are not evidence of evolution. They are evidence of creating higher costs.

BE How did you establish or promote the need for TPS to evolve?

TO In TPS, we force ourselves to see reality as it actually is, not as we hope it to be. In seeing reality, one quickly realizes that things change every day. Some daily changes are

are relevant to one's work, others are not. So sorting needs to occur, but this needs to be done carefully because some things that seem irrelevant are actually relevant. As everyone knows, I preferred to be at the genba as much as possible. While there, I issued challenges to people and I told them that I would come back sometime later to see what they had done. I established an expectation that things must change frequently and that I would follow this up with my presence. I was persistent and slowly developed their understanding in line with mine. Most managers merely utter words citing the needed for change, but they do not follow up. Therefore, it is clear that they are satisfied with the current condition. As a result, things begin to stagnate. The company becomes like a stagnant pool of water: Visibility is poor, it smells bad, it contains bacteria and parasites, it causes disease and makes people sick. Stagnation is an abnormal condition. Flowing water does have such problems.

BE Stagnation can exists in different ways. For example, a budget created in August for the coming year is out-of-date by January or February because market conditions changed. Yet, management expects everyone to adhere to the budget as if there was no change in market conditions.

TO This is why we place great emphasis in seeing reality. Otherwise, stupid things happen that cause great difficulties for many people. It forces many people to struggle as if such struggles are necessary. It is wrong to do that to people. TPS enables an organization to be flexible and adaptive to changing conditions. Plans must also be flexible and adaptable. Rigidity soon leads to stagnation.

BE Processes stagnate, and people do as well.

TO The two are related. When people stagnate they have no ideas and processes become stagnant. When processes stagnate there is no need for people to come up with new ideas. Their imagination is wiped out. They give up. Why does the company pay people who have given up? The answer is not to fire people. Management is not doing the things necessary to avoid stagnation. They must never disguise stagnation as evolution.

BE Can your meaning of evolution can be understood more simply as trying new things?

TO Yes, that is what nature does. Management must create an environment where people are comfortable to try new ideas and new methods for improving their work. Managers must be able to look at the work areas they are responsible for and describe some of the ideas that have been tried and how the process has evolved over the last few weeks or months. They must understand those details in order to know if evolution has indeed occurred. And they must recognize the ideas and process that evolved were in response to an actual need, not a made-up need. There is no sense in evolving for the sake of evolving. Evolution must occur in a manner similar to how evolution occurs in nature. Small changes based on need, made without the benefit of money or new machines. When people solve problems with money or by buying expensive new machines, it reveals that they do not understand the problem, they do not have any ideas, or they are pretending to be busy.

BE Appearances can be misleading.

TO The appearance of things being in good shape does not mean things are in good shape. A sure sign of evolution in nature is when things look different. The same is true for the workplace. If it looks different day by day or week by week, it is evolving. If it looks the same all the time, then it is stagnant.

BE In addition to evolving to keep up with the times, evolution has the added benefit of helping one to prepare for shocks.

TO Shocks to the economy or other type of shock to business are destined to occur. How do we prepare for such eventualities? Establishing TPS and evolving it forward contributes to the ability of a company to be flexible and adaptable. If you don't change a little bit every day, then you will at some point be forced to change all at once when a shock arrives. Change all at once is very difficult and disruptive. Through evolution, you control change. When a shock comes, you have no control. Imagine if you never practiced golf and were suddenly thrust into competition. You would never make it. Think of this in human terms: The way to learn golf or play piano is to practice every day. Everyone gives this same advice. It is the same advice for TPS. It is better to be prepared for shocks than surprised by them. The future will see economic shocks, technological shocks, and environmental shocks. There will be shocks from natural disasters, human migration, disease, and possibly conflict within and between nations. Business must survive these shocks with the least damage possible, and also be contributive to recovery.

BE The leaders of companies who want to avoid stagnation try to establish TPS. In addition to practicing various elements of TPS, they often import ideas from other disciplines such as industrial and organizational psychology. This includes organizational development, organizational behavior, leadership development, and change management.

TO What are these things? I have not heard of them.

BE These are different fields of academic study that seek to understand why individuals and groups do what they do in organizations. They offer theories, concepts, methods, and interventions that can help organizations overcome barriers and resistance to change. Since you are unaware of them, it is apparent that you did not make use of the findings of academic studies in these different areas.

TO That is correct. We did not use these things. I have no idea if they are effective or not. But my worry is that they could cause confusion, increase complexity, and create delays in establishing TPS. It could also introduce ways of thinking that contradict TPS. Do you know of any companies that have used these things and established TPS faster and better than those who have not?

BE No. It seems to go slower and with worse results.

TO Then why do it? As I said previously, kaizen was the method that created TPS. Toyota-style kaizen develops people, it develops organizational capabilities, it generates many improvements quickly, and it creates leaders for present and future times. So it seems to me that not much else is needed. Others can practice Toyota-style kaizen and achieve what we did. But, troubles will come when Toyota-style kaizen is altered in ways that diminish its effectiveness to simultaneously develop people and improve processes. Mostly, we carefully observed cause-and-effect in relation to people as well as processes. This guided our actions as managers. We were, of course, very interested in industrial engineering. In the early days we carefully studied the work of Frederick Taylor and Frank Gilbreth. We also studied Lillian Gilbreth's book, *The Psychology of Management*, because it was about people in relation to industrial engineering. Dr. Gilbreth's work gave us some useful insights.

BE What were they?

TO Individuality, specialization, teaching, and training methods for improving work. People today should read her book. They will find it useful. We carefully studied the old books on industrial engineering from America and tried out what we learned. We adapted what we learned from books to suit our needs. If people studied the old books, they would learn some of the ancestry of TPS.

BE It is common for companies today to try to embed the scientific method as the basic way of thinking for problem-solving. Those that seek to establish TPS typically leave out industrial engineering and Toyota-style kaizen when they train people in the scientific method.

TO This is a mistake. Both are required and both are related to each other. It is not surprising that companies struggle; that they proceed slowly and make little actual improvement. There are right and wrong ways to do things. Doing things correctly requires both careful study of the method and practice to learn the method thoroughly before one makes changes. One must not make changes to the method, Toyota-style kaizen, until the basics have been mastered. Perhaps I did not make this clear in my books.

BE It was not clear. Nevertheless, there exists a strong tendency among managers to change a method before they understand the method. By doing so, they believe bigger results will be achieved sooner.

TO Again, this is the mindset of the sprinter, like the hare. The marathoner, or tortoise, does not think this way. Perhaps my way of thinking is seen as ancient and out-of-date. We still believe that one has to learn the method through practice until it becomes instinct. Only after the basics have been mastered can changes be made. Evolution occurs based on needs, not on whims.

BE Strangely, management's efforts to avoid stagnation usually results in stagnation. It is common for managers to commit to TPS or a variant of it, yet their thinking remains unscientific and illogical; not fact-based. This accelerates stagnation.

TO At some point one has to consider the possibility of management incompetence. The money paid far exceeds the value received by the company and its employees.

BE Competent management requires development through training. In my experience, they are skilled at avoiding training that would improve their competence in the management skills required for TPS.

TO I say: Acquire management skills by training in order to take meaningful action. Management skills for TPS are completely different than management skills for conventional management. Do managers actually want to close that gap, or are they satisfied with the continued existence of the gap? What I see as abnormal, others see as normal. In this case, only one of us can be correct.

In What Ways Did This Conversation Improve Your Understanding of TPS?

-
-
-
-

How Will This Reduce Your Struggles?

-
-
-
-

School and Work

BE I seems that everyone who has gained some experience with TPS is amazed at the large gap between what they learned in kaizen compared to what they learned in school. This is true in a general sense, but particularly when it comes to critical thinking, which is the ability to discern or make judgments based on facts.

TO Of course, the big difference as it appears on the surface is book learning compared to learning at the genba. Many courses in school have a type of genba associated with it; laboratory courses and projects. Yet, these are artificial genba and not the actual genba. So there will always be a gap in the way of thinking and the learning that it produces.

BE Kaizen is by far the most effective method for developing critical thinking that I have ever experienced. As a student, I completed research projects at the B.S., M.S., and Ph.D. levels and wrote lengthy dissertations. In conventional view of education, such projects require one to ask many questions, make judgments, and come to conclusions. Answering research questions and are said to develop critical thinking skills. Indeed they do, but not nearly to the extent I experienced in kaizen.

TO In kaizen, different questions are asked compared to your research projects. Questions pertaining to the genba are practical, while questions for research projects in school are theoretical. Questions for research projects may have practical application, but the basis for inquiry is theoretical. Overall, school represents one type of learning. It builds foundations in language, mathematics, and so on. But it is a mistake to think that school is the only type of learning. If people believe that, then knowledge will be forever limited to that which aligns with what was learned in school. For example, if someone learns about economies of scale in school, then they will use that knowledge at work. They will not be interested to learn the limits of its usefulness unless they challenge what they learned in school. They must ask "Why?" and "How do I know this to be true?" Under typical conditions, work may provide 10 percent additional knowledge, or it could subtract 10 percent or more of knowledge from school education. School gives people half the education they need. TPS provides the remaining half of the education needed to make a person capable of contributing to making progress.

BE Much of formal education centers around asking "Why?" Nearly all forms of assignments and classroom discussion center on various questions. Yet, we find people tend to not ask "Why?" regardless of the setting – work or home. As a result, they are rigid in their thinking rather than flexible.

TO Progress is generated when people become dissatisfied with an existing situation. They begin to see things differently. And so they conduct experiments to determine if how they see things is accurate or not. Most people give up after one or experiments because they have encountered failure. They must be persistent. The establishment of TPS was an experiment into thinking the opposite way that others think about work, production, and management.

BE As a teacher, I find students are receptive to thinking in the opposite way. There is little resistance. Yet transferring the opposite way of thinking from the classroom to the workplace has proven to be difficult for my students.

TO There is a vast community of knowledge pertaining to 100-year old business methods. The community of knowledge for TPS is very small by comparison. There is no doubt that your students will run into all types of resistance, now and into the future. But they must persevere and find opportunities to apply what they learned and build their capabilities. They must guide themselves in the second half of their education if management will not do it. They must practice kaizen continuously to raise their skill level for cost reduction. Again, I re-iterate that cost reduction must be understood in the broad sense of total cost.

BE You say "Think like a 12-year old."

TO Yes, because that is the age where you had no preconceived notions. Education after that age builds in preconceived notions. So we must return to the age where we did not say things like "It is difficult" or "It cannot be done." Instead, we had boundless curiosity and a willingness to try things and make things. Even as adults, people like to make things. Almost every hobby you can think of involves making things. It is natural for humans to make things. Therefore, people must be allowed to try things and make things at work to generate improvements. Find a photo of yourself at age 12 and keep it nearby as a reminder of the time when you lack preconceived notions. This will help you obtain the other half the knowledge that you need.

BE You say "Do it now" and "Get it done today."

TO In school, things take too long. The teacher gives assignments that are due next week or next month. Students experience this for years. They become accustomed to taking a long time to do work or complete work, and mistakenly associate taking a long time with high quality. When they graduate and become employed, they say to their boss they will complete the task in a week or a month, or the boss gives them a week or a month to complete the task. That is no good. The understanding of time is all wrong and must be corrected. Think like a swimmer or runner; seconds count! Business is competitive; such delays cannot be permitted. Taking action is paramount. Do not spend days and weeks thinking when it is unnecessary. Spring into action! Do it now! Get it done today! Be lightning-quick, then think. It can be poorly done. Find a way quickly. You can make it better later. Improve the quality or function over time. The point is to make progress. Learn by doing to make progress. This is the other half of education that TPS gives to people.

BE You say "No conference room kaizen."

TO Conference room is like a classroom. Learning in a conference room is limited. Always go to the genba, wherever it may be, even if is a manager's office. Observe the actual work in the actual place. Don't meet in a conference room and try to recall how the work is done. See it with your own eyes.

BE You say "Don't focus on effect, focus on causes."

TO People see an effect and try to find a more efficient way to process the effect. I say understand the cause of the effect and eliminate causes. For example, a machined part often contains burrs or rough edges. People then try to find a more efficient method for removing burrs. They give this task to lower-skilled people. The machinists don't remove burrs. If you make machinists remove burrs, they will find a way to machine parts without making burrs. Why does the burr occur to begin with? No burr means no need to de-burr. Eliminate the burr from occurring. Apply this example to your situation.

BE You say "Just do it." So people follow your guidance and they are happy to have gotten something done quickly. Yet, people continue to be afraid and struggle to try things out quickly.

TO It takes dedication and practice to think like a 12-year old. It does not come naturally as an adult. To obtain the other half of education one needs is a big challenge. There is no teacher telling what to do and when to do it. You have to think for yourself. Maybe you are fortunate and have a manager that knows TPS and can guide you and instill confidence. Otherwise, the second half of your education must be do-it-yourself. The first half of your education is 15 or 16 years. The second half of your education is double that number of years.

BE You say "Don't compare before and after kaizen. Think about the next kaizen."

TO The new kaizen is immediately the old kaizen. Find new waste. In school, a completed activity is the end. This is a bad habit to learn. There is no end to kaizen. This is the good habit to learn.

BE You say "Do it lightning-quick."

TO Competition means no waiting and no delays. This applies to managers as well. Managers are responsible for as many abnormal conditions as what occurs elsewhere in the company. Managers create burrs and they leave it for others to correct. That's no good. Management's work must be designed so that it produces no burrs. It is not easy, but they will find a way. Do it now, try it out quickly, try again even if you fail 100 times.

BE Teachers in school don't teach this way.

TO Their method of teaching is effective up to a certain age and for certain subjects. Teaching methods, whether in school or in business, must reflect actual needs. The need for students is different than the need for employees. Many managers do not teach. Such managers fail in their basic responsibility to employees. Those who do teach mindlessly copy their school teachers' methods and are therefore ineffective. Managers must teach, and the teaching method they use must be based on the basic needs that exist for any business: cost reduction, productivity, and survival. And they must faithfully assure the necessary training in support of the teaching, so that employees can instinctively respond to abnormal conditions.

In What Ways Did This Conversation Improve Your Understanding of TPS?

•

•

•

•

How Will This Reduce Your Struggles?

•

•

•

•

Turning Words into Action

BE Books on TPS and its variants are sometimes criticized because they describe what to do, but not how to do it. Readers want more specific information on how to translate words into practice or action. What are your thoughts on this?

TO By now, with hundreds of books on this topic, I assume many must provide details on how to convert descriptions of TPS into practice. But even if they do not, it is up to the reader to tryout what they have read and turn words into action. It is no good to complain.

BE People want a recipe.

TO Recipes are for people who have convinced themselves that they have no imagination or who refuse to think for themselves. In doing so, they do not respect themselves; they do not respect their capabilities as humans to do great things. TPS does not follow a recipe. A recipe has many ingredients and many steps. TPS has one ingredient, kaizen, and one step, try it out. That one step leads to many other useful things. Seeking a recipe is an example of a preconceived notion. That is why I say preconceptions must be abandoned. It is impossible to establish TPS if one weighed down by preconceptions.

BE Preconceptions give people comfort and security.

TO Survival depends on discomfort and insecurity! It is foolish to expect that things come easily, with little effort.

People at work somehow expect the level of discomfort and insecurity that they experienced and became comfortable with after spending so many years in school. Business is not school! The demands on one's thinking and capabilities increases 100 times. This is why people must try things; to activate and develop their imagination and capability for thinking. This is how to contend with discomfort and insecurity. It puts you in control of your destiny.

BE Words in books should give people ideas and motivate them to try the ideas.

TO My books were intended to help people understand there is a better way to produce things. In essence, the words I wrote described the gaps that exist between TPS management and conventional management. Many of the gaps were so large that, despite my style of writing, I hoped to motivate people to learn the nature of TPS and try it out for themselves.

BE If people want to create a plan to establish TPS, they can always take the words in a book and convert them into step-by-step instructions.

TO Yes, they can do that, and perhaps it might be of some benefit to see things as a plan and performing it in steps. I cannot say for sure because I have never done that. Others should try it. But I caution you that plans tend to become fixed. A basic way of thinking in TPS is to be flexible because things change. The mere act of creating a plan establishes firm commitments. Executing a plan means that people will immediately discover defects in the plan that reduces its utility. One can continue using a plan that does not work, or one can make adjustments immediately to reflect actual results.

BE It is a curious thing that when workers show plans to managers, managers assume the plan is perfect and hold workers accountable to its exact execution. And then they blame workers when things don't go according to plan.

TO Managers should know from their own experience that plans are a representation of the future, which nobody can accurately predict. Thinking plans are accurate is a denial of one's own experience and of reality. Plans can be useful for some things, provided they are flexible. Plans tend to be applied to many more types of activities than is actually necessary, and people spend too much time updating plans every time things change. In TPS, the mindset is "try it out." That is the plan; just one step, and repeat as many times as necessary. This is the pathway to discovery.

BE These days, people learn how to create plans in elementary school. Students create plans for the day ahead, plans for writing assignments, plans for projects, and so on. This continues on through high school and college.

TO People assume 100 percent of what they learned in school is the right way to think and do things. That is a mistake. I always urge people to use their powerful brain to think whether or not a tool or method that they know how to use should be used. It is better to assume that only 50 percent of what one learns in school is the right way to think and do things. If it is more than that, then rejoice.

BE These days, people create elaborate plans for kaizen and other improvement activities.

TO Why? In the time that it takes to create plans you can try something out on the genba 10 times. We spoke of this before; the bureaucracy that is created to establish TPS. I created an autonomous study group, not a bureaucratic office to coordinate and oversee TPS activities. The key is to get people to change, and that happens when you convince people to try things. I encountered much resistance. But I found an effective way to overcome resistance was by speaking to workers at the genba, one by one or in small groups. This interaction helped me understand the sources of resistance, which I could then use to overcome resistance from other people. I did not produce a plan for whom to talk to, when to talk to them, and what to say. I just did it.

BE Workers invariably distrust management's intentions and express concern that TPS, or its variants, will cause them harm. Specifically, workers cite concerns over the possibility that TPS will de-humanize them, speed them up and burn them out, de-skill them, take away their knowledge, take away their creativity, and cost them their job. These concerns are constant over generations of workers. What are your thoughts on that?

TO Based on what we have talked about previously, workers are correct to be worried about these things. Because most managers do not understand TPS, these outcomes are likely. In the early days of TPS, we experienced some of these things, but kaizen never resulted in unemployment for anyone. For the other things, we made improvements so that these concerns were addressed. Kaizen is not just process improvement; it is improvement of humans' concerns. But this is always a moving target. Some of these concerns can pop up at any time. That is why there is no end to kaizen. People must not suffer as a result of TPS. The concerns you cite are abnormal conditions. Kaizen must be practiced to return to the normal condition, so that such concerns do not trouble anyone. When workers are troubled, management must be troubled as well. If the true nature of TPS is understood, then management and workers will work together to assure both experience the opposite of the concerns that you cite.

BE You spent a lot of time talking to people on the genba. Your words were a type of spoken "book" or audiobook that people converted into action.

TO I asked people to follow me. I did that by saying simple things that challenged people to try it out. And I followed up by asking "What is purpose?" They would explain it to me and by doing so they would experience personal discoveries and new ideas to try. I conducted quick oral exams. I did not want reports or presentations. Just go see what is happening on the genba so the manager can understand why the employee did what they did. This is the way to make improvements quickly.

BE The only record of what you actually said on the genba comes to us through the people that worked with you or whom you interacted with. It is a few things here and there.

There is no comprehensive collection of your thought-provoking wisdom.

TO That is wrong! It is not thought-provoking wisdom! It is as action-provoking wisdom!

BE Yours is an uncommon way to both teach and train in a business setting. Kaizen, patience but no patience, a focus on human development, improving and synchronizing the entire system versus the parts, total cost focus versus unit cost focus, and so on. Your words transformed into action.

TO As I have said previously, action is paramount. It must be developed into a reflex. Whether in a book or spoken, words must motivate the practice to develop the reflex for taking immediate action. At work, people spend too much time talking about things, as if there is no competition biting at your heels. People lose sight of the fact that there is competition because competitors are not physically present on the same track as runners are in a track meet. All employees must train themselves to think that way; that their competition is in the lanes next to them, and that anyone can win at any time because of the possibility of myriad mistakes than can be made in strategy and execution. Take the words to mean taking action. Action means moving forward. Moving forward means learning how to survive.

BE Taking action means to copy TPS, at least to start. There is criticism that all people do is try to copy TPS. But, if flow is the objective, then it makes sense to copy Toyota, to gain an initial foothold into methods and the way of thinking.

TO It is acceptable to copy TPS at the start if flow is the objective. If flow is not the objective, then why copy TPS? Think what happens when one learns martial arts. You begin by copying the instructor's methods and way of thinking. But, you will never progress if all you do is copy the instructor's moves and think as someone else does. You have to master the basics. Then, you have think more deeply to understand the mindset and move forward. With continuing practice, you apply your own unique ideas and creativity to improve. Over time, you evolve from copying your instructor to creating something uniquely your own. You may begin copying TPS, but through changes made over time, the T in TPS goes away and your company name replaces it. It becomes your management system.

BE It seems that the focus on waste, cost-cutting, and the harm that has come to workers who have been fired as a result of improvement has led to a change in how people teach TPS, though they may not call it TPS. And it is not always with flow as the objective. It can be other objectives. People have re-interpreted your work to focus on learning through problem-solving. Waste may or may not be part of that. The idea is to develop people and turn all employees into problem-solvers.

TO What is the normal condition if flow is disregarded?

BE Good question. I don't know. I doubt they know. It's probably be a financial objective.

TO A financial objective cannot be the normal condition for production. I should have cautioned against that. While generating profit is essential, it is partially the result of achieving the normal condition in material and information processing. The normal condition generates profit while abnormal conditions consume profit.

BE The change in focus reflects the inevitable and uncontrollable drift that occurs when things don't work out as expected.

TO It is well known that the tools and methods we use bring abnormalities to the surface so that people can identify the root cause, implement countermeasures, and quickly return to the normal condition. Of course, there is valuable learning in this. The reason to focus on waste, unevenness, and unreasonableness is to obtain cost reduction and productivity improvement. Doing so develops people and problem-solving capabilities. Changing the focus of TPS from eliminating waste to learning may be acceptable if it leads to mastery of the basics. But this is subject to criticism from managers who do not understand the connections between learning – the result of taking action – and cost reduction and productivity improvement.

BE For a few decades, it has been popular for companies to adopt TPS or its variants. To some, it has the appearance of a fad. And fads are subject to a life-cycle.

TO There can a need for popular items in one's personal life, but there is no business need for such a thing. It is stupid to manage a business based on popular movements. TPS is a management system that is flexible and responsive, and therefore puts the company on offense. With ongoing effort, it fulfills the need to strengthen competitiveness. Even though everyone looks busy, conventional management is passive. This is obvious from the amount waste, unevenness, and unreasonableness that exists. Conventional management is defensive management. The leaders of a company have choices; to manage on offense or manage on defense; to improve competitiveness or bumble along. It is impossible to imagine a company will successfully establish TPS if management adopts it for foolish reasons. Actions will be ineffective. Effort and resources will be wasted. No advantage will be gained. They may as well do something else.

BE And these days, that something else is digitization of business processes. It seems that it is easier for leaders to mandate digitizing business processes than it has been to mandate physical process improvement.

TO In the case of digitization, much of that work is done by subcontractors, whereas in the case of physical process improvement, leaders must persuade employees to change and do things differently. There is no doubt the former is much easier. But I become greatly concerned when management decides to put the company's future into the hands of subcontractors. Subcontractors' motivation for taking action can be different than that of employees. At the very least, a company must have employees with the knowledge and skills to fully understand the details of their information technology subcontractor's work.

In What Ways Did This Conversation Improve Your Understanding of TPS?

-

-

-

-

How Will This Reduce Your Struggles?

-

-

-

-

Why Not Apologize?

BE The focus of TPS on eliminating waste, cost reduction, and productivity improvement, successfully addresses the primary interests of management. The "Respect for Humanity" and human-centered nature of TPS has been largely ignored by company leaders or poorly understood. Employees, in many cases, have been harmed in various ways. As a result, they lose interest in improvement and no longer participate.

TO It is never the intent of TPS to cause harm to any anyone, especially employees. Any failure has multiple causes. Among the causes is a failure by managers to understand TPS due to a lack on hands-on practice. This proves that possessing an intellectual understanding of TPS, from reading books or listening to others, is insufficient. Managers who have caused harm to workers have also caused harm to the company. They expose the company to many problems that will prove to be costly.

BE What is the countermeasure?

TO Management must learn Toyota-style kaizen by doing Toyota-style kaizen. And they must apply what they learned in kaizen to their own work, because it too is surely plagued by waste, unevenness, and unreasonableness. Managers are very busy. But why is that? It is because they frequently overcommit themselves with many meaningless activities. They generate their own demand for work to appear as if they are busy and worth the large sum of money that the company pays them. Managers should make work   only when there is actual, verifiable demand from their marketplace, which is the employees, suppliers, customers, investors, communities, and competitors. To do this, managers must eliminate meaningless activities from their workday, lead from the genba, and periodically participate in genba kaizen. From this, they gain a true understanding of workers' struggles and the true condition of the business. Managers efforts must be focused on the actual needs of others instead of the imaginary needs of themselves or others. Please think deeply about that.

BE Managers don't want to participate in kaizen. They think it is only for the workers.

TO Such managers do not take their responsibilities seriously. So fire them! Re-hire them immediately if they commit to participating in genba kaizen. But cut their salary for the trouble they created!

BE Many organizations that have struggled or failed to establish TPS or its variants after a few years attempt to re-start their efforts. Management's efforts to re-start is met with skepticism by the workforce. What are your thoughts on this situation?

TO When managers mismanage, they must admit it and apologize to the workforce for their errors. They have created myriad abnormal conditions. In medicine, there is the phrase "do no harm." If management has done harm to people, then they must admit it and apologize.

BE Leaders don't like to apologize. They deny their mistakes and blame other people for their errors. Apologizing makes them feel less in control and less powerful.

TO Mismanagement is commonly associated with a big ego and overestimating one's knowledge and capabilities. Managers must accept the facts – the evidence that they have mismanaged – which has long been visible to everyone. If managers refuse to see the evidence, then they are fools in the eyes of those they claim to lead. They must admit they were wrong. Apologies may be unpleasant, but they are also liberating and allow one to proceed with the work that needs to be done. Apologies build or re-build trust in the management-worker relationship. Both parties are dependent on each other. Their relationship must be mutually beneficial, in pursuit of efforts to satisfy customer's needs.

BE People can be quite forgiving. Managers who are honest and humble are easier for workers to relate to and more influential as well.

TO That is why apologies are necessary to begin to rectify mismanagement. But, apologies must be followed up with consistent action over time. It is no good to apologize and continue mismanaging.

BE For the type of situation I described, what words would you use to apologize to the workforce?

TO You want me to think for others?

BE We would not want them to mismanage their apology.

You could provide a standard that they can improve upon.

TO Very well. But since I do not know any specific situation, I will provide only a general statement that expresses the basic sentiment.

> "Three years ago, I stood here and told everyone that we must adopt a new management system in order to meet the many challenges that we face in the future. We made some good progress in the first year, but faltered thereafter. We did not understand why, and in private conversations we blamed middle management, supervisors, and the workforce. We blamed everyone but ourselves. For two years, the management team was in denial that it bore any responsibility for failure. We now realize that as a management team, we did not understand our roles and responsibilities in establishing this new management system. We were not personally engaged in the processes necessary to learn how to lead and manage in the new ways. We asked you to work differently, and then we prevented you from doing that. We made many mistakes, and for that I sincerely apologize. As a management team, we are re-committing to establishing the new management system. This time, we will be enablers for you. All managers will gain the necessary knowledge of both mindset and methods through hands-on participation. We will be attentive to your needs and quickly take any required actions to support you. We hope this will re-build trust and result in mutually beneficial outcomes. Thank you for your attention."

Any manager who merely reads exactly what I have written to the workforce must be fired!

I also want people to understand two things. First, TPS is as much a state of being as it is doing. Many people copy TPS and think that appearance of TPS, evidence of its physical existence, means that they are doing TPS. If that continues, more management apologies will be necessary in the future. TPS must also exist within one's mind and be expressed in words and actions. This is true for both managers and workers. But, managers are leaders and employees follow the thinking, words, and actions of their leaders. Therefore, managers must comprehend and absorb TPS so that it becomes a state of their being. Second, managers like their processes to be quick and easy, yet they burden workers with processes that are slow and difficult. This gap must be eliminated or more apologies will be necessary. Every employee dislikes struggling to do their work. Every employee wants their work to be quick and easy, with no chance of errors or re-work. Kaizen must therefore be practiced continuously. Then, there will be virtually no need for managers to apologize.

In What Ways Did This Conversation Improve Your Understanding of TPS?

-
-
-
-

How Will This Reduce Your Struggles?

-
-
-
-

Day Five
Conversation

Automation and Kaizen

BE I'd like spend our last day together talking about the future. That includes subjects such as computers, automation, digital transformation, and artificial intelligence. Is that OK?

TO Yes. Quite a bit of my writing is in reference to the future. It is a topic that interests me.

BE Let me begin by describing a line of reasoning that has emerged recently. It says TPS is a solution for 20th century. We are now in the 21st century, so TPS no longer applies. TPS is yesterday's solution to yesterday's problems. Solutions for problems today and tomorrow require new digital technologies, not a new management technology. What do you say to that?

TO Reasoning has not occurred. Have buyers' markets gone away? Has competition gone away? Has the cost to enter a market gone away? Has innovation and the speed of change decreased? Do companies no longer want to grow? Do profits now come to companies automatically? Does waste no longer exist? Do customers no longer want what they want, as they want it, when they want it? Is it no longer important to know how to reduce costs when quantities go down? Indeed, times change, and TPS constantly evolves to keep up with the times. Throughout the years, new technologies have always been thoughtfully incorporated into TPS based on need. But the fundamental reasons for the creation and practice of TPS remain true in the 21st century as they did in the 20th century. TPS is based on realism. The need for realism does not change just because the century changed.

BE Like it or not, it seems that TPS and its variants are subject to a life cycle. Despite its merits, interest in TPS and its variants may be in the maturity or decline stage of their lifecycle. These have been with us for 30 or 40 years, so it seems only natural that interests and perspectives would change as the generations change. Of course, interests may be misplaced and perspectives could be wrong, but this seems to be the reality.

TO Perhaps that is so. The seasons come and go, and winter is inevitable.

BE So let's assume that winter is coming or that it has arrived. How can TPS and its variants that exist outside of Toyota survive through winter? What role does digital technologies such as automation play?

TO I have always been fascinated by computers. The reason why is because information flow always precedes production flow. Therefore, how computers process information, how much information they provide, to whom, when, and where is of interest. Even in the 1970s, computers were capable of providing more information than was needed. Now, there is a flood of information many times greater than in the past. Even though their costs have been greatly reduced, the information that computers produce can create costly problems. While computers are essential to business, so is the human mind. One rule must stand firm: Humans must never be controlled by computers. Realism is abandoned when computers are permitted to control people and thus de-humanize people. One must never allow that, just as one must never allow accountants to control people. Both computers and accountants run by numbers. Computer use 0 and 1 while accountants use 0 to 9. Numbers, as I have said previously, can easily deceive. They are incapable of seeing, hearing, touching, observing, judging, and so on, especially in combination with one another. TPS is a combination human information system and computerized information system. We have always been careful to assure that the correct amount of information goes to the correct place at the correct time. The timing is important, because the information is useless if it arrives early or late. It does not matter the form of the information: human, a kanban card, a display board, an adnon light, or a computer. We use different types of information in combination with one another. We do not rely on only one type of information, such as computer information.

BE The companies that make automation equipment computers, robots, software, and so on steadily advance their respective technologies. And they deploy attractive sales and marketing efforts directed towards senior managers that are very effective at convincing them to purchase or rent such items, even in the early stages when it is very expensive.

TO Since the beginning of the machine age, managers have been attracted to technologies that replace labor like a moth is attracted to a light. We do not fall into such traps easily. Such investments must be carefully considered. The considerations are more than just financial. In some cases, the job is so difficult, dangerous, or unhealthy for humans to perform that investment in new machines is an easy decision that requires no formal justification – even if costs go up, to respect the humans who do the work. In other cases, automation causes problems, such as reducing the ability to adapt or flexibly respond changes. In TPS, labor is not discharged from the company when new machines arrive. Instead, labor is re-allocated to areas in need of additional labor.

BE Long ago you advised people not to succumb to the robot craze. These days, robots cost much less and are much safer for use around humans. We are at the start of a second robot craze as well as an artificial intelligence craze.

TO Such improvements are to be expected. And investments must be made to in order to keep moving forward. But companies must not buy robots just because their competition buys robots or because robots have become fashionable. The fundamental question remains, whether today or 100 years ago: How do you make things that customers desire at a low cost? The numbers may show a quick return on investment. But have all costs been considered when purchasing robots? Or, have only those costs directly related to the purchase been considered? Justifications for purchasing automation equipment is typically based on an assumed level of production volume. If a company faces competitive buyers' markets, then actual volumes are often lower than the assumed volume. If labor costs go down but costs go up elsewhere in the company, then has a return on investment actually been achieved?

And you will surely make trouble for other managers in the company if costs go up elsewhere. One must look at these things very closely.

BE Nearly every article I read about automation and digital transformation claim great benefits and success is always certain. It is all upside and no downside. That strains credibility, in my view.

TO Of course, whoever buys automation equipment will always tell outsiders what a great success it is. By the way. I did not do that with TPS. I offered various warnings in my books. Managers are prone to falsehoods and they usually do not talk about difficulties or failures. So if you buy automation equipment based on a story in a business newspaper that reports great success, then you are a fool. You must first gather detailed information and determine if the newspaper story is true or not. Do not rely on sellers or second-hand information; go see for yourself and give thorough consideration. Never assume what you read in the business newspapers about automation technologies is true. People want to you buy things that you don't need. Keep this foremost in your mind. What it is that you need? Perhaps nothing. Buy only what you actually need, not what others tell you that you need, or what is fashionable, or simply to consume available budget. This is how to make things at a low cost.

BE If I may summarize: Your advice is to avoid investment based on fads, keep up with automation technologies in relation to actual needs, and make decisions based on thorough knowledge of all costs. In addition, always keep this question in mind: How do you make things at a low cost?

TO Yes, whether the thing made is a product or service, low total costs. The same question applies to both. Use your intelligence to make good, fact-based decisions at the right time.

BE You always caution people against doing things that restrict the ability to be flexible and adaptable to changing times. How does that apply to automation?

TO If you have antiques in your home, you are seen by your visitors as sophisticated. If you have antiques at work, you are seen by visitors as stupid and backwards to the times. Perhaps not. There are stories about Toyota using old equipment into early 1980s. It is foolish to think it was that way everywhere in the company. The equipment we used met needs and resulted in low costs. We did not buy machines merely for the sake of buying machines. That is how you increase costs. Automation equipment must be carefully scrutinized to determine if it has more features than needed, if it can be used flexibly, or if their use causes constraints that prohibit improvement. Machines are often designed in ways that purposefully create constraints and cost more because they contain unnecessary features. You can easily accept that. Or, you can do as we do. We work with machine and software suppliers to eliminate or reduce the constraints, eliminate features to take cost out, and then make our own customized modifications to improve flexibility. One of our long-held objectives has been for engineers to develop their engineering skills on-the-job by modifying machines to improve their flexibility or making machines to suit a particular purpose. Engineers who simply buy machines from catalogs turn themselves into uninformed shoppers and quickly lose their engineering skills. The same is true for other things such as automation and information technology. One's skills must evolve and improve through hands-on modifications and improvement, and by making things.

BE And this is how you kept up with evolution in computer and automation technologies.

TO It is a mistake to think that TPS has a reflex that instinctively rejects new machine technologies. TPS, equipment, methods, learning, and so on co-evolved in step with one another between the late 1940s through 2000. Are things different because the year changed to 2001 and we entered the 21st century? No. The difference is we challenge each other to use our intelligence to ensure that we do not increase costs to the company. This is not just a question for production. Any department has this same challenge. If you use your intelligence in this way, intelligence grows. Over time, this becomes another source of competitive advantage.

BE In what ways do investments in automation effect the practice of kaizen?

TO Automation and sensors introduce changes to the human-machine interface. The changes could be better or worse. The challenge is to discern the actual changes to the human-machine interface, and not just take the word of the seller that it is better. This is why kaizen never ends. It is possible to purchase or rent new equipment that makes it difficult to eliminate waste and improve processes. This must be avoided. Kaizen must never be sacrificed for the sake of installing new automation equipment. The two must co-exist. There is no guarantee that new machines will eliminate waste, unevenness, and unreasonableness. The likelihood is that they will increase waste, unevenness, and unreasonableness if used as directed by the seller or if used improperly. Even today, most machine makers do not understand waste, unevenness, and unreasonableness. They design their products according to their way of thinking, not our way of thinking. I have seen many cases where new technologies reduce productivity, especially in office work. One must never forget that Toyota-style kaizen was developed and has always been practiced in relation to the combinations of work performed by humans and machines. For as long as there is people in the workplace, kaizen must be practiced to answer the fundamental question that everyone must ask: How do you make things at a low cost?

BE These days it seems as if the pace of change is faster than ever. That any business can be disrupted by automation, software, and various other technologies.

TO Toyota-style kaizen trains people how to understand work and quickly make improvements. The need to do this does not evaporate simply because we have entered a new century or because new automation technologies come along. Again, I say: Use your intelligence to make good decisions at the right time.

BE The variants of TPS have a different approach to kaizen, one that does not work very well. Improvement is slow, complicated, bureaucratic, and not much fun.

TO Automation does not automatically improve things. Nor do sensors. They can slow work down by creating bottlenecks in various places. They can increase output to amounts that far exceed that which has actually been ordered by customers. This is why kaizen must become like a reflex. If you are at home and you have an idea, you try it out immediately. This is the mindset that people must have at work. And management must vigorously support and do it themselves. Not only are improvements made quickly, it gives people more satisfaction from work and strengthens competitiveness. If companies do kaizen in a way that matches its slow pace, then they obtain almost no advantage, and bottlenecks caused by automation will persist. Kaizen becomes useless and is ineffective at training people to do things quickly in an era where rapid change is common across nearly all industries. Because Toyota-style kaizen improves one's thinking and reflexes for quick action, I believe it is the future of work.

In What Ways Did This Conversation Improve Your Understanding of TPS?

-

-

-

-

How Will This Reduce Your Struggles?

-

-

-

-

Human and Artificial Intelligence

BE Your writings reflect a tremendous faith in human intelligence, both as individuals and in teams. You developed an effective method to steadily cultivate that intelligence over time. Today, people might say that change is occurring too rapidly these days to develop human intelligence as you did decades ago. How do you respond to that?

TO I have faith in human intelligence because I have seen people do amazing things; they did things that they never imagined they were capable of doing. While it does take time to develop human intelligence to a full capability, humans are not idle; they are making improvements ever day. Human intelligence is being developed in-time with actual improvements that are needed when they are needed. The argument that change is occurring too rapidly these days to develop human intelligence is nonsense.

BE Sometimes people say such things as a way to convince decision-makers to adopt new technologies that they are selling. These days, artificial intelligence technologies are becoming a more common feature in business. Such arguments are presented to position AI as a labor-saving technology that will help businesses reduce their costs. This will likely be an effective way to sell AI systems, and labor is likely to be displaced.

TO As with any technology, management must investigate it thoroughly and understand its effects on labor and many other factors. One must not simply assume that labor is no longer needed as a result of artificial intelligence. Questions must be asked such as: How can labor displaced by AI be re-allocated for different purposes? How can labor be used in combination with AI to greater effect? How will customers respond if labor is replaced with AI? Does AI increase or decrease total costs? Questions such as these must be asked before managers make decisions to eliminate labor from the company. Customer's wants and needs are ever-changing. It is more likely that the company will need the labor and must re-allocate it within the company to achieve growth or other important objectives. That will have greater benefit to the company than the savings generated from terminating employees.

BE As you said earlier in our conversation about automation and digital transformation, management must respect humans.

TO Managers have many wildly incorrect ideas about "Respect for Humanity." For example, they think it is corporate altruism, or that it is optional to the discretion of individual managers or the company as a whole. "Respect for Human" is a business necessity. Isn't it true that the human brain is still the most formidable computer? Computers can do calculations much faster than humans. But machines are limited in their ability to synthesize information and produce judgments or make decisions. Of course, these limitations will recede over time. AI is a computer, and computers lack the human touch. The human touch remains a necessity in business, within company activities and external to it in relations with customers, suppliers, investors, communities, and even competitors, as these parties work with one another to achieve shared objectives in pursuit of mutually beneficial outcomes. They type of human touch that each party seeks changes over time. Take the example of customers. It may be acceptable for some types of human touch to disappear, such as with self-service. But a time may come soon after a self-service feature is accepted by customers that they no longer accept it. Things change quickly. So management must be prepared for realities such as this. Replacing employees with AI could turn out to be an expensive mistake. I believe it is a certainty that AI and employees must co-exist because the combination of these two intelligences will result in a level of responsiveness to changing times that is greater their either one can achieve alone. Since its inception, TPS has demonstrated how humans and machines can co-exist and co-evolve in beneficial ways to both and in relation to satisfying customers' needs. The same will be true as the use of AI becomes more prevalent in business. The question is, how will management make use of it? The various options must be carefully considered.

BE There is growing consensus among business leaders that AI cannot replace human creativity and problem-solving skills, and these skills we be in demand for many years to come.

TO Perhaps this is true. However, if human creativity and problem-solving skills are thwarted by managers due to bureaucracy or company politics, then they may as well fire all employees, including themselves, and let AI take over the business. Nearly all managers say they want human creativity and problem-solving skills, but their actions rarely match their words. The establishment and evolution of TPS proves that for many decades, Toyota managers actively develop and make practical use of human creativity and problem-solving skills. This occurs on a daily basis, not just when the company gets into trouble. AI processes information in a cold, indifferent way, but humans process information in a warm, empathetic way, and provide insight and wisdom. Humans are creative, curious, ask questions, challenge paradigms, have ideas, collaborate, work in teams, conduct experiments, interpret data, and make decisions. They advise, coach, motivate, nurture, make sense out of complex conditions, determine strategies and tactics, and so on. And humans can think in two directions: forward reasoning, how causes lead to effects, and backwards reasoning, from effects to causes. Forward reasoning is prediction, which is of limited value. If I am not mistaken, AIs capability is forward reasoning. Managers who rely on predictions are bound to run into troubles. Backwards reasoning is a required skill in TPS and of great value. Managers focus their coaching on developing this skill in employees because it is a powerful source of learning and thus an excellent source for cost reduction.

BE TPS has long shown these uniquely human characteristics to be valuable in business. Managers interested in AI are now forced to comprehend what you have long understood. They are coming to a view that it is important to respect humans.

TO It is distressing that such recognition has come so late in the practice of management. We have been saying this and evolving our understanding and practice of "Respect for Humanity" for several decades. Managers did not learn this from us, their human peers. Now they will they learn it from AI, a machine? I am skeptical that words extolling the virtues of uniquely human characteristics will be matched by actions. Time will tell.

BE AI has the potential to refine management practice in ways that other efforts have largely failed. It seems that these uniquely human characteristics – creativity, experimentation, and so on – are increasingly becoming a requirement.

TO They were a requirement in the past as well. I see many companies where, over the years, management has developed a bias against workers. They are considered nothing more than a cost, are seen as troublesome, demanding in various wants and needs, and so on. Suddenly, workers are no longer seen that way? Why? It is possible that this sudden new view of workers is merely a cover to aid the introduction of AI and gain acceptance by current workers, while the real intention is to eliminate workers in the future? As I said before, I am skeptical. Though, I hope to be proven completely wrong. We have always viewed employees as valuable resources. They have imagination. AI does not. They are the endless fountain for identifying abnormal conditions and generating myriad ideas for improvement. AI does not make improvements, people do. Kaizen will remain a valuable method in the age of AI, and perhaps beyond.

BE In our previous conversation you said: "Because Toyota-style kaizen improves one's thinking and reflexes for quick action, I believe it is the future of work." Can you please elaborate on that?

TO Prior to times of rapid change, as well as during times of rapid change, employees must be trained continuously in how to think and quickly take action. The training associated with conventional management does not do that. If people react quickly, it is almost always based on poor information, hunches, data that has been manipulated, and the like. Kaizen prepares people for many things, including how to rapidly respond in times of rapid change. Kaizen trains people out of complacency and into a state of action based on the needs of the times. Kaizen teams are quickly formed, disbanded, and re-formed to meet the ongoing challenges of the work they are engaged in. Toyota-style kaizen is training for the information age. It utilizes all of the unique human characteristics and capabilities that machine intelligence lacks. Computers cannot identify what needs to be improved. Perhaps someday, AI will do that. But for now and the foreseeable, future humans fulfill that role and also take the practical action necessary to make improvements.

BE Kaizen teams are the "first responders" to business problems; to abnormal conditions.

TO All employees must think and act like first responders when abnormal conditions arise. Machine vision can assist humans in identifying defects and other abnormal conditions, but in a limited way. While managers may be tempted by AI to eliminate people, they risk eliminating those who can respond best to the need for immediate action and process improvement. This should make economic sense to managers from both a cost and revenue perspective. Machine intelligence is complacent and cannot execute immediate improvement. It is likely that managers will blindly rely on prediction machines simply because they paid for it and they believe expensive machines to be more capable than humans. This is why I say proceed with AI, based on need, and use human intelligence to make good decisions at the right time. Do not let machines decrease the company's flexibility. Customers want companies to be flexible, and flexibility is a capability that improves competitiveness. Let us not forget that kaizen, which is commonly understood in terms of cost reduction, also contributes to sales growth. In increasingly competitive markets, managers must think of Toyota-style kaizen as a way to achieve sales growth.

BE And people enjoy kaizen!

TO It is a mistake to think that kaizen is a 20th century practice that has no use in the 21st century. Kaizen is necessary whether the era is analog or digital. This is a fact. Kaizen is forever. Nowhere does it say that kaizen ends because AI begins. Waste did not go away when computers arrived, and introducing AI in a company will not make waste suddenly go away. If the AI machine tells you to stop kaizen, you must ignore it. It is not as smart as you think.

BE There is a simple economics associated with AI just as there is with economies of scale. It is thought that machine intelligence, whose strength is prediction, will reduce the cost of goods and services. The reasoning is that the supply of goods and services relies on prediction; that there is no better way to determine production than by prediction.

TO That such foolish ideas endure is remarkable. The use of forecasting is well-known in business, whether it is human intelligence alone, a combination of human intelligence and computer, or, computer alone. This works if a company supplies a sellers' market, where you can sell everything you make. It may work in cases where competition is concentrated among a few companies and whose actions are more like a cartel than competitors. In this case, they will try to restrict output in order to raise process and obtain higher profits. No matter what the scenario, sellers' markets, whether naturally occurring or created artificially, will displease customers sooner or later. Customers will look for and find alternative means to satisfy their needs. Management's efforts must be directed at pleasing customers. One effect AI is already having is to inform customers of the range of choices that are available to them, instead of customers having to labor to find a few choices that are available to them. AI could backfire and undo management's best efforts to create sellers' markets so they can sit back and relax while the money rolls in. But buyers' markets are the dominant market, so one must produce according to demand and find methods to do so at low cost, versus relying on high volumes as the means of achieving low unit costs. Predictions are for those who believe in the fantasy of sellers' markets, or that sellers' markets last forever. Buyers' markets require producers of goods and services to make what is required, in the amount required, when it is required. At the level of annual sales, we rely on prediction. It is called "sales projection." We know its value is limited and that it would be foolish to produce according to the annual sales forecast because we don't know what customers actually want until they tell us. But, as the time comes closer to production, we move steadily from high uncertainty forecasts to lower uncertainty forecasts to production based on actual demand.

BE The simple economics argument suggests that better prediction capability from AI will reduce inventories, improve inventory management, and increase the accuracy of demand forecasting. Machine intelligence will improve over time and replace human prediction.

TO Managers will be attracted to AI for all of the bottom-line enhancing promises made by sellers. But, if you overproduce because the predictions are off, have you actually reduced costs and improved productivity? If your production system is slow to respond to changes in the marketplace, have you actually reduced costs and improved productivity? The use of AI to predict these things will remain limited for some time to come because customers change their minds. They react to many unexpected events, singly and in combination, such as new entrants to the market, discounts, recessions, natural disasters, fads, and so on. Autonomous driving is a successful application of machine intelligence because roads don't change, though hazards do. As the machine learns, it will get better at predicting how humans react to hazards. Will the same be true for the "hazards" related to the production of goods and services? Perhaps in time it will. In the interim, AI could drive companies into bankruptcy due bad predictions resulting in overproduction or underproduction. Both are a loss to the company and society.

BE This is why you say make only what is needed when it is needed. Sell one, make one. Companies go broke based on bad predictions of customer demand. Just-in-Time avoids this problem and also results in low costs.

TO I believe in the age of AI, it is likely that you will continue to see slow moving items put on sale, the continued existence of so-called dollar stores who buy a company's overproduction for a fraction of the cost to produce it, and so on. This will be good for customers, but bad for companies as profits will suffer. TPS is a way to more closely match supply and demand, and ensure that both seller and buyer receive value that makes both happy. It is difficult to do this, and good quality information is essential. That is why I have always been interested to see the evolution in computing capability and software development. It is a pathway for improving the realization of just Just-in-Time. This has long been apparent to me. So while others use information in the hope of making better predictions, better prophecies, our use of information is to establish facts and take concrete action based on facts.

BE The sales-to-inventory ratio in the United States has steadily remained at a level of between 1.25 to about 1.35 for all businesses, and higher for retailers than manufacturers and wholesalers. That means there is roughly 25 to 35 percent more inventory than sales, and as high as 50 percent depending on where a company is in the supply chain.

TO And where does all that inventory go? In warehouses. E-commerce offers many benefits to customer, but currently the solution for quick order fulfillment is to build hundreds of massive warehouses to store items. The vast majority of items held in warehouses are slow-moving. Instead of Just-in-Time, the e-commerce system is evolving in the direction of fewer inventory turns – fewer information turns – and forcing various companies in supply chains to carry costs for long periods of time. While e-commerce seems fast to the customer, there is a lot of slow activity going on in the background. And some companies are being crushed by the costs they must bear until payment is made. The debt they incur is not free. There is no doubt in my mind that some manufacturers, warehouse owners, logistics companies, and others will go broke under this arrangement.

BE So you're vision for e-commerce is that the information age should result in the ability to more precisely respond to buyers' markets and actual customer demand, rather than perpetuate sellers' markets and making predictions of customer demand.

TO Yes. Predictions lead to more warehouses, more inventory, and fewer inventory turns. As AI is applied to the current e-commerce system, the effect will be to improve the efficiency of a structurally inefficient system where many people hold big investments and fear losing their money. Perhaps the AI machine's voice will become brave and yell out to top managers what a mistake it is to build more warehouses. I believe TPS shows the way forward for business in the 21st century.

In What Ways Did This Conversation Improve Your Understanding of TPS?

-
-
-
-

How Will This Reduce Your Struggles?

-
-
-
-

Final
Thoughts

Final Thoughts

BE Our time together is coming to an end. You have been very generous in answering my many questions.

TO I am known for doing the opposite. Because of our conversations, people may think I have become softer and sweeter. But, let us look at things more closely. The apparent situation is that you have asked questions and that I have provided answers. The actual situation is that I have provided guidance and correction. Readers must ask their own questions and discover their own answers by trying things out for themselves.

BE The objective of this book was to introduce or re-acquaint people with the work you did to establish TPS, the true nature of TPS, and how TPS is a management system for the digital age. Because people are more familiar with the work of others who interpreted TPS, I feel our conversations will be a great help to those who want to improve their understanding of TPS and reduce their struggles to practice TPS.

TO I want to again emphasize the need to try, even if you fail 100 times. Do it, then think. This means to experiment and understand the result. Don't give up. Waste is infinite. TPS does not come easily, but it is necessary.

BE I think readers can now better understand that the thinking and methods that were developed and evolved in the 20th century apply in the 21st century as well. The usefulness of TPS is expanded by information technologies, not diminished by it.

TO That is how I see it. Because TPS evolves in step with changing times, changing needs, changing markets, and changing technologies, it continues to be relevant. I think I have now made this very clear: TPS is the management system for the information age. We have spoken much about action and taking action. I would like to provide additional guidance on this point.

BE Please do.

TO In English, the work "action" means to accomplish something. This is not specific enough. People can take action and do things that are not necessary. This is not what I mean by action. Action must always be in reference to the normal condition. The Plan-Do-Check-Act cycle has the following meaning: Plan is set-up. Do is do. Check is to determine if a gap exists between what was expected to happen, the normal condition, and what actually happened, an abnormal condition. Act means kaizen. Use kaizen to close the gap and bring the process back to the normal condition. All employees, from president to workers must recognize and correct the gaps between what they expected to happen and what actually happened. These gaps occur every day, often many times a day, no matter what one's work is. All four steps of the P-D-C-A cycle must be one quickly! The cycle is not completed in the time-scale that one learns in school and which has become one's habit. The time-scale habit for business is hours and days, not weeks and months. You must break the bad habits you learned in school and replace them with good habits.

BE So people should use the word "kaizen" instead of "action." The Plan-Do-Check-Kaizen cycle. P-D-C-K, to return to the normal condition.

TO Yes, always use the word "kaizen" instead of "act." "Kaizen" means improvement, "act" does not. As we conclude, I also want to clarify the meaning of other words such as creativity, human intelligence, and idea generation. I want to make sure that my meaning becomes the reader's meaning. TPS will never be established if people apply their own meaning to things.

BE Or their old habits, which count among the preconceptions that must be abandoned.

TO Many people believe they are not creative. This is nonsense. Their understanding of creativity is based on preconceptions. They think of painters, illustrators, musicians, people who write novels, and so on. In order bring people's innate creative abilities to the surface for TPS, one must focus on a simpler meaning of creativity as *ideas*. When people recognize a gap between what they expected to happen and what actually happened, they must learn to ask "Why?" Managers must develop people so that asking "Why?" becomes an instantaneous reflex This is the beginning of kaizen. When people ask "Why?" they start to uncover answers to their questions. These answers generate ideas for them to try. Trying generates many more ideas to try. In this way, people exhibit vast creativity without realizing it. This is how TPS is established.

BE But you impose constraints on people so that they do

not rely on preconceptions to close the gap and bring the process back to the normal condition.

TO Yes. I require them to use their brains, human intelligence, not money. They must spend ideas instead of money. We teach everyone to think as craftsmen do when it comes to using one's human intelligence; their ingenuity. A craftsman is someone who loves their work and who typically struggles to get by. They always face gaps in their work between what they expected to happen and what actually happened. Because they are struggling to get by, they have no money. They can either spend their savings or borrow money to correct problems. Neither is attractive to craftsmen. So they have to use their intelligence and ingenuity instead of money. They make do with what they have, such as basic hand tools and small power equipment, and find things in their shop or in the junkyard for little money or for free that they can use to improve the process and return to the normal condition. And because of limitations in resources, improvements must be simple. In doing this many times – by trying again and again – the craftsman gains skills and develops wisdom that improves their ability to close gaps in ever-more ingenious ways that cost no money. And, as a result of daily practice, they are able to do this more quickly and more effectively. In time, they develop a level of mastery that enables them to train others to develop their own ingenious ways of closing gaps.

BE Do you have any final thoughts for managers?

TO Gaps between what is expected to happen and what actually happens are ever present in everyone's work – top managers to workers on the line. TPS is based on realism and personal responsibility. If managers and others ignore the gaps in their work and proceed as if everything is fine, then the basis for their work is fantasy and personal irresponsibility. This cannot be the basis for providing customers what they want according to individual needs. When the basis for management's work is fantasy and personal irresponsibility, then they fall prey deceptions caused by numbers, appearances, and so on. Flow can never be achieved under such circumstances. And it will not be long before the company lands into trouble. Management is entrusted with the responsibility to not land the company into trouble. It is expensive to get out of trouble; management wastes company money to get out of trouble that should never have happened, and workers often bear the consequences of managers who believe in fantasies and lack personal responsibility. Of course, managers are humans and they make mistakes, but the number of mistakes must be small and none should be severe. That is the target condition that management must establish for itself. It is based on realism and requires acceptance of personal responsibility.

In What Ways Did This Conversation Improve Your Understanding of TPS?

-

-

-

-

How Will This Reduce Your Struggles?

-

-

-

-

Further Reading

Books by Taiichi Ohno

Toyota Production System: Beyond Large Scale Production
Productivity Press, Portland, Oregon, 1988

Workplace Management
Productivity Press, Cambridge, Massachusetts, 1988

Just-In-Time for Today and Tomorrow
with Setsuo Mito Productivity Press, Cambridge,
Massachusetts, 1988

See Taiichi Ohno in:

NPS New Production System: JIT Crossing Industry Boundaries
Isao Shinohara, Productivity Press, Cambridge,
Massachusetts, 1988, pp. 141-159

Also see:

"On The Tabletop Improvement Experiments of Japan,"
Alan Robinson and Margaret Robinson, *Production and
Operations Management*, 1994, Volume 3, Issue 3,
pp. 201-216

About the Author

M.L. "Bob" Emiliani is a professor in the School of Engineering, Science, and Technology at Connecticut State University in New Britain, Conn., where he teaches a course on leadership, a unique course that analyzes failures in management decision-making, as well as other courses.

Bob earned a Bachelor of Science degree in mechanical engineering from the University of Miami, a Master's degree in chemical engineering from the University of Rhode Island, and a Ph.D. degree in Engineering from Brown University.

He worked in the consumer products and aerospace industries for 15 years, beginning as a materials engineer. He has held management positions in engineering, manufacturing, and supply chain management at Pratt & Whitney.

Bob joined academia in September 1999. While in academia, he developed the Lean teaching pedagogy and led activities to continuously improve master's degree programs.

Emiliani has authored or co-authored 17 books, four book chapters, and more than 45 peer-reviewed papers. He has received six awards for writing.

Visit www.bobemiliani.com and www.leanprofessor.com

www.ingramcontent.com/pod-product-compliance
Lightning Source LLC
Chambersburg PA
CBHW031930190326
41519CB00007B/470